mind's
Talk for Writing

Andrew Hammond

CONTENTS

How to use this pack	2
Core Learning for Literacy	3
IMAGES: Teacher's Notes and Photocopymasters 1 – 20	4
SOUNDS: Teacher's Notes and Photocopymasters 21 – 25	44
Cross-curricular links to QCA Schemes of Work	64

RISING STARS

PRINCIPLES OF MIND'S EYE TALK FOR WRITING

This resource recognises the importance of Talk for Writing and the need to embed teacher and pupil talk in all stages of the teaching sequence.

The **stimuli** (sounds and images) along with the **introduction** are particularly supportive of whole class teaching and learning, whilst the **writing activities** and **photocopymasters** are particularly suited to supporting guided and independent writing.

This resource also offers support for the hardest parts of writing and turns pupil 'talk for writing' into *the* writing.

HOW TO USE MIND'S EYE TALK FOR WRITING

Preparation and planning

Use the chart on p3 to check out which unit fits with your planning requirements in terms of the core learning in literacy from the Primary Framework.

Use the chart on p64 to check out the range of genres, text types and cross-curricular coverage of your chosen unit.

Read the Teacher's Notes to make selections and personalise for the needs of your class as appropriate.

Select the writing activity you want to focus on or decide which groups will work on which writing outcomes.

Photocopy the student activity sheet as appropriate (photocopymaster).

Bring up the unit image or sound file and 'hide' using the hide and reveal tool on your interactive whiteboard.

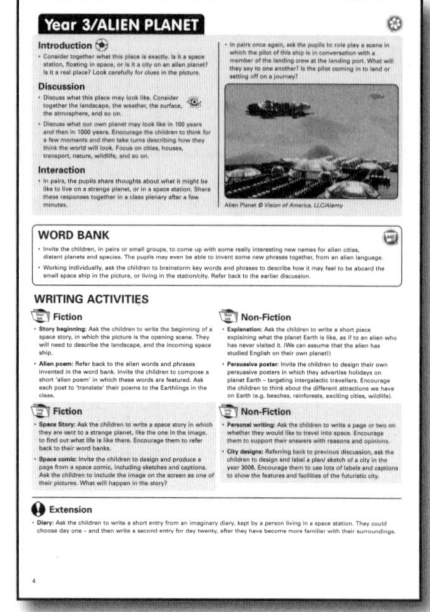

Use the *Mind's Eye Writing Year 3* CD.

Ask children to consider an image in their mind's eye.

The hardest parts of writing:	Mind's Eye Talk for Writing Suggested lesson sequence:
Having the ideas and enough ideas to sustain the writing.	**Introduction** 1. Capture interest with image or sound. 2. Talk about the image or sound. 3. Activate prior knowledge from pupils. 4. Encourage an open-ended eliciting and development of response. **Discussion** Use 'teacher talk' prompts to stimulate group or class discussion. **Interaction** Ideas for setting up a range of oral paired activities and small discussion groups to capture the ideas and rehearse these.
Using good vocabulary and achieving expression.	**Word Bank** Topic-related vocabulary and specific spelling rules and conventions that will complement and develop the pupils' knowledge and expertise. Practising these ideas and rehearsing them ensures that pupils are not hindered by a lack of the basics when they begin writing.
Shaping the whole and using appropriate and varied sentences.	**Writing Activities** For each unit, eight writing activities are suggested; two short activities for both fiction and non-fiction and two longer activities for both fiction and non-fiction. In each case teacher prompts are provided to ensure that the teaching sequence for writing is maintained: 1. Familiarisation with the genre/text type 2. Capturing ideas/oral rehearsal in line with the task 3. Teacher demonstration 4. Teacher scribing/supported writing/guided writing.
Independent writing	The outcome of each writing activity along with the use of the photocopymaster provided supports the pupil in independent writing.

CREATIVE THINKING (YEAR 3)

The introductory sessions, word bank activities and writing activities in *Mind's Eye: Talk for Writing (Year 3)* all help to raise standards in writing through the promotion of creative thinking. In the publication *Excellence and Enjoyment: Learning and teaching in the primary years* (DfES 0518-2004G) creative thinking is identified as a key aspect of learning. It involves the children in:

- generating imaginative ideas
- discovering and making connections
- exploring and experimenting
- asking questions
- trying alternative or different approaches
- looking at things from other points of view
- making connections and seeing relationships
- reflecting critically on ideas, actions and outcomes.

These strategies are incorporated into each unit in *Mind's Eye: Talk for Writing (Year 3)*.

CORE LEARNING FOR LITERACY – STRANDS AND OBJECTIVES (YEAR 3)

From Primary Framework for Literacy and Mathematics 02011-2006BOK-EN

Core learning in literacy strands for Year 3 (numbers correspond to paragraphs/points within each strand)

Mind's Eye Images Unit	1 Speaking	2 Listening and responding	3 Group discussion and interaction	4 Drama	6 Word structure and spelling	7 Understanding and interpreting texts	8 Engaging with and responding to texts	9 Creating and shaping texts	10 Text structure and organisation	11 Sentence structure and punctuation	12 Presentation
ALIEN PLANET	3, 4	1	3	1	3			2, 5	1	2	
BUTTERFLY	2	2				1, 3		3, 5	2	2	2
CHINESE DANCER	3	1	1, 3	1	1	3, 5	3	2, 3	1	2	
CLIFF HANGER	3, 4	1	2, 3	1, 2	3			2, 3, 4	2		
DRAGON	1, 3	1	1, 2	1, 3	3	3	3	2	2	2	
FIRE BRIGADE	3	2, 3	2		3			4	1, 2	1, 2	1
FISHING NET	2, 3	1, 2	3	1	2, 3			2, 3	2		
HIGH SEAS	3, 4	1	1, 3	1, 2, 3	1, 2	1, 3		3, 4			
IN THE SPOTLIGHT	2	1	1	1, 2	1			3, 4		2, 3	
KITTEN	1	1	2		1			2, 3	1	2	2
MESSAGE IN A BOTTLE	4	1	2, 3	2		1, 3		3		2	
OFF-ROAD DRIVER	3	3	2	1, 2	3		3	3, 5		3	2
PARACHUTE JUMP	1	1	3		2	5	3	1, 3	1	2	2
PARTY TIME	3	1	2, 3		1	3		2	1		
PYRAMIDS	2, 3	1	3	1, 2	2			1, 2		2	
RACING DRIVER	1	1	3	2	1	3		2, 3	1	1, 2	
RAINY STREET	1	1	2		1			2, 3, 5	2	2	2
ROBOT WORLD	3	1, 2	3			1, 3	2	2, 4	1, 2	2	
THE GIANT	3	1	2		3	3, 4, 5	3	1, 3		2	2
WATERFALL	3, 4	1	2, 3		1, 2, 3	3	3	3	2	2	

Core learning in literacy strands for Year 3 (numbers correspond to paragraphs/points within each strand)

Mind's Eye Sounds Unit	1 Speaking	2 Listening and responding	3 Group discussion and interaction	4 Drama	6 Word structure and spelling	7 Understanding and interpreting texts	8 Engaging with and responding to texts	9 Creating and shaping texts	10 Text structure and organisation	11 Sentence structure and punctuation	12 Presentation
CAVE ATMOSPHERE	1, 3	1, 3	2		1			3	2	2	
COUNTDOWN TO LIFT-OFF	3	1, 2	3	1, 2		3	3	2, 3	2		2
FIREWORKS	2, 3	1			1, 3	3		3, 4	2	2	2
HORSE RACE	1	1	2, 3	1, 2, 3	1	5	3	2, 3		2	1
JUMBO JET	2, 4	2, 3	1, 2	1, 3				3	2	2	
RING THE ALARM!	3	1	2		1	3		2, 3		2, 3	
RIVER FLOWING	3	1	2		1	1		1, 2, 3	2	2	
ROYAL FANFARE	3	1	3		3			2	2	1, 2	
THUNDERSTORM	3, 4	2	2, 3		1, 3	3, 4		3, 4, 5	2		2
TIGER GROWLING	1	1	3			5		1, 2, 3	1	1, 2	

Year 3/ALIEN PLANET

Introduction
- Consider together what this place is exactly. Is it a space station, floating in space, or is it a city on an alien planet? Is it a real place? Look carefully for clues in the picture.

Discussion
- Discuss what this place may look like. Consider together the landscape, the weather, the surface, the atmosphere, and so on.
- Discuss what our own planet may look like in 100 years and then in 1000 years. Encourage the children to think for a few moments and then take turns describing how they think the world will look. Focus on cities, houses, transport, nature, wildlife, and so on.

Interaction
- In pairs, the pupils share thoughts about what it might be like to live on a strange planet, or in a space station. Share these responses together in a class plenary after a few minutes.
- In pairs once again, ask the pupils to role play a scene in which the pilot of this ship is in conversation with a member of the landing crew at the landing port. What will they say to one another? Is the pilot coming in to land or setting off on a journey?

Alien Planet © *Vision of America, LLC/Alamy*

WORD BANK
- Invite the children, in pairs or small groups, to come up with some really interesting new names for alien cities, distant planets and species. The pupils may even be able to invent some new phrases together, from an alien language.
- Working individually, ask the children to brainstorm key words and phrases to describe how it may feel to be aboard the small space ship in the picture, or living in the station/city. Refer back to the earlier discussion.

WRITING ACTIVITIES

Fiction (Short task)
- **Story beginning:** Ask the children to write the beginning of a space story, in which the picture is the opening scene. They will need to describe the landscape, and the incoming space ship.
- **Alien poem:** Refer back to the alien words and phrases invented in the word bank. Invite the children to compose a short 'alien poem' in which these words are featured. Ask each poet to 'translate' their poems to the Earthlings in the class.

Non-Fiction (Short task)
- **Explanation:** Ask the children to write a short piece explaining what the planet Earth is like, as if to an alien who has never visited it. (We can assume that the alien has studied English on their own planet!)
- **Persuasive poster:** Invite the children to design their own persuasive posters in which they advertise holidays on planet Earth – targeting intergalactic travellers. Encourage the children to think about the different attractions we have on Earth (e.g. beaches, rainforests, exciting cities, wildlife).

Fiction (Long task)
- **Space Story:** Ask the children to write a space story in which they are sent to a strange planet, like the one in the image, to find out what life is like there. Encourage them to refer back to their word banks.
- **Space comic:** Invite the children to design and produce a page from a space comic, including sketches and captions. Ask the children to include the image on the screen as one of their pictures. What will happen in the story?

Non-Fiction (Long task)
- **Personal writing:** Ask the children to write a page or two on whether they would like to travel into space. Encourage them to support their answers with reasons and opinions.
- **City designs:** Referring back to previous discussion, ask the children to design and label a plan/ sketch of a city in the year 3006. Encourage them to use lots of labels and captions to show the features and facilities of the futuristic city.

Extension
- **Diary:** Ask the children to write a short entry from an imaginary diary, kept by a person living in a space station. They could choose day one – and then write a second entry for day twenty, after they have become more familiar with their surroundings.

Name _____   Date _____

THE SPACE HOTEL

Who knows, perhaps in years to come we shall all be enjoying holiday trips into space, to stay in space hotels!

But what would a space hotel look like? What sort of things would it offer its guests? Think about bedrooms, food, games, sport, leisure and entertainment.

Design a brand new space hotel and then label it to show all the things that it offers. You could name it after yourself!

The _____ Space Hotel

© Rising Stars UK Ltd. 2007   Mind's Eye/Writing   Year 3/ALIEN PLANET

Year 3/BUTTERFLY

Introduction
- Identify the type of insect this is and discuss its features.
- Elicit the children's knowledge and experiences of butterflies. Where do you usually find them, and at which time of year?

Discussion
- Discuss together the question: *If you could be any insect, which would you be, and why?* Ask the children to think for a minute or two and then share their thoughts, justifying their answers with reasons and explanations.
- Discuss together how a butterfly is formed. You may wish to refer to books or websites for accurate information. Demonstrate the process on the board, or invite the children to explain the process to the class, using diagrams and sketches. Identify the key points in the explanations given.

Interaction
- Consider together how beautiful this butterfly is. Then invite the children in pairs, to make a list of other animals and insects which they consider to be beautiful. Share these in a plenary. (You may wish to distribute animal books first.)
- Play 'word tennis', in which two volunteers sit at the front of the class and reel off as many different animals or insects as they can, in a category which you may give them: e.g. *sea animals, birds.* The person who cannot think of a new answer is out.

Butterfly © INSADCO Photography, Alamy

WORD BANK
- Consider together how a butterfly moves. Come up with an appropriate verb or doing word (e.g. *fluttering*). Then ask the children, in pairs, to make a list of animals and write an appropriate verb next to each one, e.g. *tiger – prowling, salmon – leaping, snake – slithering.* Share answers.
- Can the children spell the insects that they know? List all the insects you can think of and check the spelling of them using dictionaries and spell-checkers. You could play insect bingo!

WRITING ACTIVITIES

Fiction (Short task)
- **Rhyming poem:** Ask the children to compose their own short poems about a particular animal or insect. Encourage them to use a rhyming scheme (e.g. a, b, a, b). You could begin by modelling a short class poem on butterflies.
- **Descriptive writing:** Ask the pupils to write a descriptive paragraph about the first time they saw a butterfly. If they cannot remember, then they may invent descriptions. Encourage them to focus on its bright colours, its movement and the way they felt when they first saw it fluttering by.

Non-Fiction (Short task)
- **Factual descriptions:** Ask the children to write a short factual description of the butterfly, for someone who has never seen or heard of one. Share these in class. Then repeat the exercise for e.g. *a spider* or *a moth.*
- **Labelled diagram:** Using books, magazines or Internet sites, the children research then design and annotate their own diagrams of the features of a butterfly, and then present this information to the class. This may be done using ICT to develop keyboard skills and extend experience of graphics.

Fiction (Long task)
- **Fantasy story:** Invite the class to write stories about giant insects and animals. What might happen if they came across a butterfly with a six foot wingspan, or an ant as big as a dog? Share plans then encourage them to get writing!
- **Writing in role:** Ask the children to plan and draft diary entries, writing as the butterfly in the picture. What happens in the day in the life of a butterfly?

Non-Fiction (Long task)
- **Personal writing:** If the children could fly, like a butterfly, where would they most like to go? What would they most like to see? Ask them to write down their thoughts in a page of personal writing.
- **Persuasive writing:** Lead a brief discussion about how precious the insects, birds and animals are around us. Then encourage the children to write a short piece in which they persuade readers to look after their garden wildlife.

Extension
- **Research:** Invite the children to research the different kinds of butterflies in the world. They may draw sketches of a few kinds and then produce some accompanying text, which lists e.g. habitat, diet, size, etc. This may also be done using ICT.

Name _____   Date _____

I'VE GOT BUTTERFLIES!

Have you ever heard someone say 'I've got butterflies?' Do you know what it means?

It actually means that the person feels nervous. There are plenty of other funny sayings which we sometimes hear. Can you write down what these animal phrases actually mean?

I've got a frog in my throat.

_____

He's like a bear with a sore head.

_____

She eats like a bird.

_____

He is barking up the wrong tree.

_____

She is a busy little bee.

_____

I worked like a dog today.

_____

© Rising Stars UK Ltd. 2007   Mind's Eye/Writing   Year 3/BUTTERFLY

Year 3/CHINESE DANCER

Introduction
- Where do the children think this picture might have been taken? How do we know it may not be in this country?
- Look for clues in the picture: the architecture, traditional costume, girl's nationality. Establish that it is in China, at the Tiantan Gate, Beijing.

Discussion
- Elicit the children's knowledge of China. Where is it in the world? What do we know about China? Establish some basic facts on the board, drawing information from the children.
- Discuss together why this girl may be dancing on the steps of this building. Is it a large festival or other event? Suggest theories. Invite the children to imagine the rest of the scene (*other dancers, musicians, spectators, dragons*).

Interaction
- In pairs, invite the children to consider what type of building this might be. Ask them to write down different uses for it and then feed back to the class in a final plenary. Suggestions might include: *temple, concert hall, palace*. Check spelling of terms on the board.
- Hot seating: Invite volunteers to take the role of the dancing girl in the image and sit in the hot seat to field questions about why she is dancing and what kind of festival it is.

Chinese Dancer © *Vision of America, LLC/Alamy*

WORD BANK
- Ask the children, either in pairs of individually, to imagine that this is part of a large religious event in Beijing. Can they write down words and phrases to describe the atmosphere at the scene? Encourage them to think about the music, other sounds, sights, smells and mood of the crowd. Share words in class, and monitor spelling.
- What other sorts of dancing can one enjoy? Disco dancing, ballroom dancing, ballet dancing? Ask the children to work in small groups, writing down the names and types of dancing they can think of.

WRITING ACTIVITIES

Fiction (Short task)
- **Descriptive writing:** Can the children imagine being in the square in Beijing when a large festival is on? Refer back to the earlier discussions, and the word banks. Then ask them to write a paragraph or two to describe what the event might be like, focusing again on the atmosphere.
- **Poem:** Discuss how the children feel when they dance. Do they feel happy, excited and free, or do they feel a bit embarrassed or nervous? Ask them to write a short poem about dancing.

Non-Fiction (Short task)
- **Advertising poster:** Ask the children to design and produce a poster, advertising a dance festival in their town. Discuss together the venue, date, time, entertainment, food and so on. Perhaps it could be a Chinese dance festival! Identify features that will provoke readers' reactions.
- **Dance outfit:** Ask the children: What would your favourite dance outfit look like? Draw an outfit and then label it. Write descriptions for the outfit. The pupils present their designs to the class.

Fiction (Long task)
- **Adventure story:** Ask the children to focus this time on the building in the background of the picture. What could this be? Ask them to write a story in which they go to China and discover an extraordinary building. They enter and explore it. Encourage them to describe the walls, roof, windows, decorations, interior.
- **Festival story:** Invite the pupils to plan and draft a short story about a festival that is to be staged in their town. What sort of things will it offer? What will the weather be like? Encourage them to describe and narrate the event, in chronological sequence.

Non-Fiction (Long task)
- **Personal writing:** Ask the children to think about an event or festival that they have attended at some time. What was it celebrating? Can they remember some of the sights, sounds and smells they experienced at the time? Encourage them to write about their experiences.
- **Personal writing:** Refer the children back to the discussion about China. If they could visit any country in the world, what would it be, and why? Ask the pupils to write down their thoughts in a piece of personal writing.

Extension
- Ask the children to look again at the image and to imagine they are an emperor or empress, arriving home at their palace, after a long spell away. The flags are out and the dancers and musicians are here. Write about their royal welcome home!

Name _____ Date _____

POSTCARD FROM BEIJING

Imagine you are visiting Beijing during a family holiday in China. You decide to write a postcard home to a friend.

Describe the dance festival in the square, outside the beautiful temple. Think about the sights, sounds and smells of the place!

In the spaces below, draw a picture for the front, and write a message on the back. Don't forget to put an address too!

© Rising Stars UK Ltd. 2007   Mind's Eye/Writing   Year 3/CHINESE DANCER

Year 3/CLIFF HANGER

Introduction
- What on earth is this man doing?! Does anyone know?
- Share the children's reactions to the idea of abseiling. Would anyone like to try it when they are older?

Discussion
- Sustain a conversation in which the pupils share their views on extreme sports like this. What other exciting pursuits do people engage in? (Write these down.) Why do they do it? Have any of their parents or elder siblings done something like this?
- Discuss together where this photograph may have been taken. Encourage the pupils to picture the landscape and then describe it to the class.

Interaction
- In pairs, the children come up with some interesting speech or thoughts for the person in the photograph. What is he thinking as he goes over the edge? Feed back after a few minutes.
- Hot seating: Invite volunteers to take turns in sitting in the 'hot seat' and fielding questions from the class in the role of the climber in the picture. Encourage interesting questions about his motivation etc. Where else has he climbed? How does he feel when he abseils?

Cliffhanger © Ingram Publishing/Alamy

WORD BANK
- Ask the children to make a list of the kind of equipment (i.e. common nouns) that they might use in sports of this kind. They can begin with what they see in the picture. Share ideas and check spelling by writing the nouns on the board.
- In pairs, ask the children to write down describing words (adjectives) that capture how they might feel in this climber's position. Share these at the end. You could start them off with: *excited, nervous, brave*.

WRITING ACTIVITIES

Fiction (Short task)
- **Postcard:** Invite the children to write their own fictional postcards home, after a day's climbing and abseiling in a place like the one featured in the picture. Encourage them to refer to their word banks for interesting adjectives.
- **Descriptive writing:** Discuss again what this person might be able to see from the top of this mountain/cliff. Ask the children to write this down in a descriptive paragraph, focusing on: the landscape, weather, atmosphere, the sheer drop. Again, encourage the use of interesting adjectives.

Non-Fiction (Short task)
- **Sounds:** Ask the children to write a short paragraph describing the kinds of sounds you might hear on a mountain side like the one featured in the picture (e.g. the wind, birds, mountain sheep, aeroplanes, nervous breathing).
- **Poster:** Ask the children to work in pairs for this task. On a sheet of A3 paper, they must design a fun poster promoting a particular extreme sport. Refer back to the list from the discussion above.

Fiction (Long task)
- **Climbing story:** Ask the pupils to plan and draft a story of their own in about an exciting adventure rock climbing on a mountain. Will something go wrong, perhaps? How will the characters feel? Encourage the pupils to use the lists of words from earlier sessions.
- **Adventure story:** Invite the children to write a different story, in which the main character(s) enjoy some abseiling in a very unusual place – e.g. down the side of a city building, the Eiffel Tower, or a church steeple.

Non-Fiction (Long task)
- **Recounts:** Ask the children to write an imaginary recount of a mountain expedition. They may include a route map of the climb up the mountain, and then refer to how they felt at each stage. Brainstorm words and phrases to help them, like time connectives and personal pronouns.
- **Personal writing:** If the children could do any of the extreme sports you have discussed, which would it be, and why? Invite them to write down their choice and their reasons.

Extension
- In the future, what kind of weird and wacky things will we do in the name of sport? Will it be rock climbing on the moon? Or underwater chess? Invite the children to think of one or two ideas and then explain them, with sketches and diagrams.

Name _____   Date _____

DON'T LOOK DOWN!

Can you imagine being the person in picture?
Would you look down?

Here are some interesting adjectives that you might find in a poem all about climbing. See if you can use them to write a climbing poem all of your own.

| thrilling   cold and windy   exciting   scary |
| challenging   fun   adventurous |
| sharp and jagged   tiring   peaceful   quiet |

A Climbing Poem

_____
_____
_____
_____
_____
_____
_____
_____
_____

Year 3/DRAGON

Introduction
- Ask the children: 'What type of creature is this?'
- Elicit the children's knowledge of dragons. Where have they seen them – in books, on films, in other places? Are there any famous stories about dragons that they know?

Discussion
- Is this creature real or fictional? If no one has ever seen a dragon in the flesh, does this mean they don't exist? Share ideas and thoughts about dragons.
- Consider all the stories, myths and legends about dragons. Why are we so fascinated by them? Are all dragons alike in the myths and legends, or do they differ?

Interaction
- In small discussion groups, invite them to come up with theories about where this dragon has come from and where it is going. Is it being chased? Has it seen its prey? Share theories in a class plenary.
- In pairs, encourage the children to act out a short scene in which one of the children returns home excited about having just seen a dragon. The other is a family member who takes some convincing. Share, and critically appraise, pupils' performances.

Dragon © Christian Darkin/Alamy

WORD BANK
- Dragons often feature in myths and legends. What other words and phrases do we sometimes find in stories of this kind? Discuss with the children the language of myths and then, in groups, encourage them to write down as many of these words and phrases as they can, e.g. *sword, shield, gods, good and evil, love*. Share these in class.
- Encourage the children to work in pairs, recording interesting adjectives to describe this dragon, e.g. *shiny, scaly, gigantic*.

WRITING ACTIVITIES

Fiction (Short task)
- **Acrostic poem:** Remind the children what an acrostic poem looks like. Then set them the task of writing an acrostic poem using the key word DRAGON. Brainstorm interesting words and phrases first, referring back to the word bank above. Invite the pupils to perform their poems aloud.
- **Descriptive writing:** Ask the pupils to write a paragraph of descriptive writing about the dragon in the picture. You could focus thoughts on: appearance, movement, behaviour, feelings (including hunger!). Make special mention of the consistency and presentation of handwriting.

Fiction (Long task)
- **Myths and legends:** Ask the children to write a myth or legend of their own about a dragon, referring back to the word bank above. Discuss the importance of having a hero and a villain, an interesting setting and some magic too. Consider the features of myths that provoke readers' reactions – e.g. fight against evil, empathy for hero's plight.
- **Adventure story:** Invite the pupils to write a story in which some characters discover an extraordinary creature deep in a jungle. It could be a dragon, or it could be something else entirely new. How will the people react?

Non-Fiction (Short task)
- **Personal writing:** Ask the children to think about what it might be like to fly on the back of the dragon in the picture. Where would they go? Who might they visit? Invite them to write half a page explaining where they would go and what they would do if they could hire a dragon for a day!
- **Design a dragon:** Invite the children to think of designs for their own dragon. What sort of features would it have? Then ask them to draw their chosen dragon and label it. Each child may then present their dragon design to the class.

Non-Fiction (Long task)
- **Information text:** Ask the children to invent their own facts about dragons and present this in an information text, or non-chronological report, with diagrams, sketches, labels and captions. You may like to look at similar texts for crocodiles, dinosaurs etc. for ideas about layout.
- **Newspaper headline:** Ask the children to imagine that a dragon has been spotted flying above their own town. Then invite them to write the front page of a newspaper, reporting the amazing story, using eye-catching headlines and introductions. ICT may be used.

Extension
- **Personal writing:** Dragons have a magical talent for breathing fire. But what special powers would the children like to have? Would they too like to breathe fire? Or become invisible? Discuss and then share thoughts in writing.

Name _____   Date _____

A LOT IN COMMON

Dragons may seem strange, magical creatures, but they share a lot in common with many real animals. Just think about it.

Can you work out what these animals all have in common with the dragon in the picture? The similarities are listed below. Choose the right one for each animal.

ANIMAL	SIMILARITY
BAT	
DINOSAUR	
CROCODILE	
LIZARD	
EAGLE	

SIMILARITIES

They both have wings.

It has claws, just like a dragon.

They both have scales on their skin.

Both animals are gigantic.

They both have a tail.

© Rising Stars UK Ltd. 2007   Mind's Eye/Writing   Year 3/DRAGON

Year 3/FIRE BRIGADE

Introduction
- Look carefully at the details in the image. What do the children think is happening here?
- Elicit the children's knowledge and experience of the fire service. What do they do? What sort of emergencies do they attend? Discuss the role of a fire officer.

Discussion
- Discuss why these fire officers may have been called to the scene. What could be happening that needs so many fire fighters? Can the children take any more clues from the picture, e.g. the giant ladder?
- Look closely at the dials and switches on the left of the picture. What are these for? What might the boxes and crates on the right of the image be storing?

Interaction
- Ask the children to record, in pairs, all the different sorts of emergencies a fire fighter might be called to – from a cat stuck in a tree, to a blazing house. Share these in class. Focus attention on the fire brigade's equipment and skills.
- Working in small groups, the children discuss together which emergency service they would most like to work for, giving reasons for their answer. Share these in class.

Fire Brigade © *Vision of America, LLC/Alamy*

WORD BANK
- Ask the children to write down the names of all the emergency services we have in this country – e.g. police, fire brigade, ambulance service, air sea rescue, mountain rescue, lifeboat, etc. Then check the spelling of each on the board. Have they spelt them correctly? Which words and letters caused particular confusion (e.g. *ambula*nce, *mountain*)?
- Ask the children to write their own individual lists of equipment a fire officer might need when called to a fire. Then share lists in class. Examples will include: *hose, ladder, helmet,* etc. Check spelling of each.

WRITING ACTIVITIES

Fiction (Short task)
- **Poem:** Ask the children to draft a short poem about a fire fighter. Refer the children back to the discussions you have had, and the word banks they have compiled.
- **A day in the life:** What do you think a fire officer gets up to each day? Is one day ever the same as the last? Share ideas and thoughts, then ask the pupils to write a fictional diary excerpt, describing a typical day for a fire fighter.

Fiction (Long task)
- **Descriptive writing:** Invite the children to write a descriptive paragraph about what they think is actually happening in the image, perhaps from the viewpoint of the fire fighter in the foreground of the picture.
- **Adventure story:** Invite the children to write a story in which the fire brigade are called out to an emergency. What has happened? Describe the fire fighters and the work they do to save the people involved.

Non-Fiction (Short task)
- **Instructional poster:** Ask the children what they know about what to do if a fire breaks out either at home or at school. Discuss the important steps necessary. Then ask them to produce their own fire safety instruction poster, informing younger children what to do in case of fire, using ICT.

Non-Fiction (Long task)
- **Design a fire engine:** Invite the children to design their own futuristic fire engine. What will it be able to do? What kind of features will it have? Using an A4 sheet, the children sketch the vehicle and then include lots of labels and captions.
- **Incident report:** Invite the children to imagine that they are the fire fighter in the foreground of the picture. Ask them to write a brief report to describe what they did when they got to the scene of the emergency. This may then be presented formally to the class, and critically appraised – on language, sequence and delivery.

Extension
- **Information text:** Invite the children to find out more about what the fire brigade do for us. They may use books, magazines and Internet sites to locate some interesting facts. Then ask them to present this information using pictures, diagrams, labels and captions.

Name _____ Date _____

ARE YOU BRAVE ENOUGH?

What sort of qualities do you think you need to become a good fire officer? Think about it.

Write down some words that describe what sort of person you think you need to be to join the fire brigade. The first two have been done for you.

_____   _____

_____   _____

_____   _*strong*_

_____   _____

*fearless*   _____

_____   _____

Year 3/FISHING NET

Introduction
- Ask the children where they think the boy is. How can they tell? How old is he?
- Ask the pupils if they can identify what is in the background of the picture. Could this have been taken in this country? What is the weather like?

Discussion
- Discuss the children's experiences of visiting beaches. What sort of things might they find washed up on a beach when the tide has gone out?
- Share ideas about what the boy may have caught in his fishing net. You may wish to list these suggestions on the board, using a brainstorm map or spidergram.

Interaction
- Invite volunteers to come and sit in the 'hot seat' and answer questions from the other pupils in the role of the little boy in the photograph. Questions could relate to who is with him, what he has found, how he feels, etc.
- In groups, the pupils consider what this boy might be thinking at the moment. Ask each group to come up with a line or two of speech to accompany this photograph, like a speech bubble.

Fishing Net
© Image 100/Alamy

WORD BANK
- Working in pairs, the children make a list of verbs that you might associate with the beach: e.g. *beachcombing, running, fishing*. Share these in class and compile them on the board, to show the spelling. Focus on the application of –ing endings.
- In groups, the pupils make another list of the items (nouns) one might find on a beach. Then ask them to write down one adjective for each noun, e.g.: *rickety deck-chairs, salty seaweed*. You may wish to focus on alliterative phrases here.

WRITING ACTIVITIES

Fiction (Short task)
- **Postcards:** Ask the children to write, and illustrate, a postcard from the little boy, describing what he has been up to, and what he caught in his fishing net.
- **Descriptive writing:** Ask the children to think about what this boy can see to his left, right and in front of him. Then ask them to write a short descriptive paragraph about the landscape. Remind them to think about their senses when imagining the scene.

Fiction (Long task)
- **Fishing trip:** Ask the children to plan and draft a story in which a boy or girl on a fishing trip catches a most unusual item in their net! The settings for the stories may be the seaside, or a river, or lake, etc.
- **Story beginnings:** Practise writing story openings based on the theme of the seaside. Discuss different ways of beginning a story, e.g. character dialogue, description, etc. Then ask the children to write half a page for three story openings. Share these in a class plenary.

Non-Fiction (Short task)
- **Instructions:** Ask the children to write a list of instructions reminding readers how to behave when they are on a beach – think about health and safety, keeping clean and tidy, respecting others' privacy, and so on. Discuss the use of bullet points and illustrations.
- **Equipment list:** Invite the children to write an equipment list for a good day out at the beach. Discuss together the kinds of things they might need and then ask them to write these down clearly and with accompanying illustrations. Invite the children to present these to the class.

Non-Fiction (Long task)
- **Newspaper report:** Invite the children to write a newspaper report entitled *BOY FINDS TREASURE ON BEACH*. What sort of treasure could he have found? Discuss the features of journalistic recounts including, facts and names, eyewitness accounts, time references, chronological accounts, etc.
- **Advertisement:** Ask the children to design and write a newspaper advert advertising a holiday resort by the sea for a 'grand day out'. Mention activities, location, etc. Consider design and layout together.

Extension
- **Personal writing:** Ask the children to think about why so many of us like to spend time at the seaside. Ask the pupils to write a short piece, explaining why they personally like, or dislike, the seaside.

Name _____   Date _____

BEACHCOMBING POEM

Write an acrostic poem all about a day at the seaside. Think about what you might find if you could spend a whole day beachcombing in the sunshine!

Remember, in an acrostic poem, the first letter of each line forms part of a word – this time, it's BEACHCOMBING.

B _____
E _____
A _____
C _____
H _____
C _____
O _____
M _____
B _____
I _____
N _____
G _____

© Rising Stars UK Ltd. 2007   Mind's Eye/Writing   Year 3/FISHING NET

Year 3/HIGH SEAS

Introduction
- Have the children ever seen a ship like this before?
- Discuss together how old this ship might be. How does it compare to modern ships today?

Discussion
- Elicit the children's experience of tall ships. Where have they seen them before – in books, in films, in naval museums? Imagine together what it must have been like to work on such a ship. What sort of jobs would they have had to do on board?
- Who is our most famous admiral? What do the children know of Horatio Nelson? Share knowledge and experience.

Interaction
- Ask for volunteers to take turns in assuming the role of the ship's captain. Invite them to sit in the 'hot seat' at the front and answer questions from the class, staying in character.
- Invite the class to imagine they are members of the crew, on a voyage to discover new lands. In pairs, the children role play a conversation. It is their first night on board and they feel apprehensive! Share performances and appraise each other's work, focusing on gesture, action and dialogue.

High Seas
© John Henshall/Alamy

WORD BANK
- Divide the class into groups and give each one a large sheet of paper and marker pen. The pupils brainstorm all the words and phrases they can think of to describe life on board this ship. Share ideas in a plenary.
- Discuss together how soft letters and blends – like *s* and *sh* – are often used in poems and stories about the sea. Brainstorm some good examples of 'sea' words beginning with the letter *s*. (e.g. *soft, silky sand, shimmering, salty seaweed*, etc.).

WRITING ACTIVITIES

Fiction (Short task)
- **Sea poems:** Write a class poem together on the theme of the sea. Use some of the 'soft' sounding words from the word bank. Focus on the sights, sounds and smells of the ocean. Then invite the pupils to plan and draft their own sea poems. Share them in a final plenary.
- **Descriptive prose:** Individually, the children write a paragraph of descriptive prose in which they describe the appearance of the ship in detail. They may choose to write from a sailor's point of view.

Non-Fiction (Short task)
- **Annotations and captions:** Ask the children to draw their own tall ship and then use annotations and captions to label its different features. Then ask them to draw a futuristic ship for the year 2106. Encourage them to label their drawings carefully, using short, factual descriptions.
- **Reference text:** Consider together what sailors might have taken with them on a long voyage many years ago. Then invite the children to write an equipment list for a modern sailing trip. What would the children take with them?

Fiction (Long task)
- **Information text:** Ask the children to write a double-page spread from an imaginary information book on the theme of sailing boats through the ages. Encourage the class to research this topic first, using books, magazines and websites.
- **Letter:** Ask the children to write a letter as one of the sailors on board ship, to their family back home. Remind them that this will be in the first person narrative, and will include some personal thoughts and feelings about life on board.

Non-Fiction (Long task)
- **Sea adventure story:** Discuss together what makes a good sea story. List some of the features and characters one might find in stories of this kind – e.g. *pirates, stormy weather*, etc.). Then ask each pupil to plan and compose their own sea story, featuring the ship in the picture.
- **Dialogue:** Ask the children to write a passage of dialogue in which members of the crew discuss plans to lock up the captain and take over the ship (mention the term *mutiny* here). Invite the children to read their work aloud in groups.

Extension
- **Recount text:** Ask the pupils to write a fictional journal, or captain's log, in which they recount life on board, as the captain of the tall ship in the picture. Remind them to write in the first person narrative, recounting events and experiences from the captain's own viewpoint.

Name _____ Date _____

SEASIDE SYNONYMS

Synonyms are different words that share the same or similar meaning – like *big/huge* or *wet/damp*. Synonyms help us to avoid using the same word too many times in a story or poem.

Can you think of some interesting synonyms for the following seaside words? Remember to try to keep the same meaning. You might need to use a thesaurus.

1. cold _____ 4. windy _____

2. warm _____ 5. hungry _____

3. pebbles _____ 6. exciting _____

Now see if you can fill in the gaps in the following sentences with a synonym that means the same as the word in brackets.

1. The captain _____(*shouted*) at his lazy crew.

2. When the sun went down, the sailors felt _____(*sad*) and homesick.

3. The men were _____(*angry*) because the captain would not let them have a _____(*rest*).

4. On the horizon they could see a _____(*beautiful*) island.

© Rising Stars UK Ltd. 2007   Mind's Eye/Writing   Year 3/HIGH SEAS

Year 3/IN THE SPOTLIGHT

Introduction

- Where is this picture set? How can we tell it is on a stage? Refer to the curtains, the spotlight, the dark boards, etc.
- Elicit the children's experience of being on stage. Can they remember what it felt like?

Discussion

- Discuss together what might have happened on this stage moments after the photograph was taken. Could this have been the beginning or the end of the show? What type of show?
- Share experiences of visiting a real theatre. What have the children seen? Did they enjoy the experience?

Interaction

- In pairs or small groups, the children role play a short scene which shows us what was about to happen on the stage when the photograph was taken. It could be the opening scene, the interval, or the finale, for example.
- In pairs, ask the children to consider what sort of talents they have and what they would do for an audience if they had to spend two minutes in the spotlight. Share these answers in class. Consider what a talented class you have!

In the Spotlight © Comstock Images/Alamy

WORD BANK

- What are the words and phrases we tend to associate with live theatre? Ask the children to brainstorm these, either in pairs or as a class on the board. Anything relating to the theatre will do, e.g. *props, lights, greasepaint, wings*.
- How many names of shows do the children know? In pairs, invite them to make a list of all the stage productions, past and present, they can think of. Familiar ones to start them off are: *The Lion King, Peter Pan, Oliver*.

WRITING ACTIVITIES

Fiction (Short task)

- **Introduction:** Invite the children to imagine a show that is about to take place on the stage in the photograph. Ask them to think about how they might introduce this show to the audience. The children then write such a speech and share it in class.
- **Descriptive writing:** How would the children feel if it were they who were about to walk through the curtains and appear on stage in front of a live audience? Ask them to write about a moment when they face all those eyes watching them – this could be based on real experience or pretend.

Fiction (Long task)

- **Playscript:** In pairs, the children prepare a very short piece of drama which could be performed on a stage just like this. The theme could come from a current history topic, or anything else, e.g. fire fighting, sailing, or visiting a haunted house! Ask them to write down their script so that they can then perform it in class.
- **Story:** Ask the children to write a story about a musical or dramatic show that goes badly wrong, e.g. scenery collapses, someone faints or falls in the orchestra pit, etc. After a few minutes, share the first few lines of some stories together.

Non-Fiction (Short task)

- **Personal writing:** Ask the children to produce a short piece of personal writing about what was the most enjoyable live performance they have ever seen. Can they describe the event and why they enjoyed it so much?
- **Advice:** Remind the children that lots of people feel nervous when they are on stage. But how do we all cope with nerves? Do we take a deep breath, count to 10, or something else? After a discussion, ask them to design a poster, giving advice on how to beat stage-fright and stay relaxed.

Non-Fiction (Long task)

- **Personal thoughts:** Begin another discussion about feeling nervous. This time ask the question: When else do we feel nervous in life? E.g. at the dentist, before a spelling test. Invite the pupils to write about when they feel nervous, giving reasons why they do and how it feels.
- **Production advertisement:** Ask the children to design and produce an advertisement (on an A4 sheet) for an imaginary musical or dramatic production at a theatre.

Extension

- **Personal writing:** Explain that there are lots of people involved in most stage productions, and not all of them are on stage – e.g. directors, make up artists, etc. Invite the children to write about which would be their favourite job in theatre, and why.

Name _____   Date _____

I SAY! I SAY! I SAY!

Do you know any jokes? Sometimes it's very hard to remember them isn't it? But you would not want to forget them if you were a comedian on stage!

Write down three of your favourite jokes in the spaces below, then learn them off by heart. You can pretend you are on a stage, entertaining a huge audience (which could be your class!).

Joke no. 1

_____
_____
_____
_____

Joke no. 2

_____
_____
_____
_____

Joke no. 3

_____
_____
_____
_____

Year 3/KITTEN

Introduction

- If many of the children say 'ahhh!' discuss why they did this. Why do we often react in this way to a picture of a kitten?
- Extend the discussion to cover how this image makes us feel. Encourage the children to come up with some words and phrases to describe their emotions, and record these on the board, e.g. *happy, sympathetic, soppy*.

Discussion

- Consider together what has caught this kitten's attention? Divide the class into pairs and invite each pair to come up with their own theory, which is then shared in class.
- Is this a common colour for a cat? What sort of colours do you see? Elicit the children's own knowledge and experience of kittens and cats. Encourage them to describe their own cats at home – colours, characteristics, behaviour, and any funny anecdotes.

Interaction

- In small groups, the children discuss together why so many people have cats as pets. If there are members of the group who do not like cats, can they explain why they don't?
- Ask the children the question: if you could have any animal for a pet, what would it be, and why? In a circle, take turns in sharing your preferences.

Kitten © Juniors Bildarchiv/Alamy

WORD BANK

- Can the children think of words and phrases to describe this kitten – both its appearance and its character? The children may work in pairs or small groups. Share feedback at the end. You may wish to start them off with: *cute, curious, delicate, pretty*.
- Ask the class to think of all the kinds of pets people have at home. Then ask them to write down ten of them, and think of a really good adjective to put alongside each one. E.g. *peaceful fish, boisterous puppy, cheeky hamster*. Share work. Are some describing words better than others? Why?

WRITING ACTIVITIES

Fiction (Short task)

- **Poem:** Invite the children to write an original poem about the kitten in the image. Encourage them to think carefully about its behaviour as well as how it looks.
- **Thoughts:** Ask the children to imagine that they are the kitten in the photograph. Invite them to write a paragraph describing what they are thinking at this moment, using the first person narrative.

Fiction (Long task)

- **Adventure story:** Invite the children to plan and draft a story about a beloved cat that goes missing. How do the owners feel? What adventures might the cat get up to? Encourage the pupils to think about the sequence of events in the story.
- **Animal story:** Ask the children to draft a different story, this time featuring the kitten in the picture, and writing it in the first person narrative, as the kitten. Where has it been, where is it going?

Non-Fiction (Short task)

- **Poster:** Invite the pupils to design and produce a poster in which they offer readers advice on 'how to look after your cat'. You may wish to begin with a brief chat about food, bedding, etc. Remind them to use visual images and text (using ICT).
- **Explanation:** Ask the children to imagine they are working for a company producing children's nature encyclopaedias. Their task is to write an entry for 'cats'. They must explain what they look like, their diet, behaviour, and so on. They are writing for someone who may never have seen a cat.

Non-Fiction (Long task)

- **Information text:** Discuss other members of the cat family (e.g. lions, tigers). What are the differences and similarities between a lion and its distant cousin, the domestic cat? Ask the children to present this information in a text, with a big cat on one side and a domestic cat on the other. Remind them to use images, labels and captions.
- **Newspaper feature:** Ask the pupils to write an imaginary newspaper feature, describing a cat that has gone missing, asking people to look out for it, and offering a reward to anyone who finds it.

Extension

- **Persuasive writing:** Ask the children to decide whether they prefer cats or dogs as pets, then write a short persuasive speech, in which they give reasons for their choice. Hold a debate in class: cats or dogs for the best pets?

Name _____ Date _____

EASY LIFE...

It's not a bad life if you're a cat! Just think about it. A good nap, some breakfast, another nap, perhaps a little stroll around the garden. Not bad.

Describe a day in the life of a cat, using the storyboard below. Include pictures and then write a sentence or two underneath each one to explain what the cat is doing.

© Rising Stars UK Ltd. 2007

Mind's Eye/Writing   Year 3/KITTEN

Year 3/MESSAGE IN A BOTTLE

Introduction
- Ask the children where this picture might have been taken. How do they know it is at the coast?
- Establish what it says on the message, and discuss the shapes. Could these be countries? What does X mean?

Discussion
- Elicit the children's knowledge and experience of messages of this kind. How do they travel? Where could this one have come from? And why?
- Consider the person holding the bottle. Who might this be? A tourist on holiday? Perhaps a life guard on patrol?

Interaction
- Invite individual volunteers to come to sit in the 'hot seat' to answer questions from their peers in role as either the person holding the bottle, or the person who wrote the message (of course, it could be the same person!).
- Working in pairs, ask the children to come up with their a new theory about where this message has come from and who might have written it. Then invite them to explain their ideas in turn.

Message in a Bottle © *Steve Hamblin/Alamy*

WORD BANK
- Ask the children to imagine they are stranded on a desert island. They can send a message out to be rescued, but they must only use ten words. Repeat the exercise with 5 words, then 3, then 1. They will have to choose their words carefully. Share ideas in class.
- If the children found themselves stranded on a desert island, how would they feel? Would these feelings change as time went on? In small writing groups invite the pupils to brainstorm adjectives to describe they would feel: a) on arrival, b) after a week, and c) after a year.

WRITING ACTIVITIES

Fiction (Short task)
- **Senses poem:** Working in a circle, invite the children to close their eyes and imagine they are on a desert island. What can they hear, smell, see, taste and touch? Then ask the children to write their own poems, entitled *Alone on an Island*, in which each of five verses covers a different sense.
- **Dear diary...** The pupils imagine they have been shipwrecked on a desert island. The only things they have with them are paper, pencils and a book. They begin a diary, in which they can record how they feel. Write out 'Day One'.

Fiction (Long task)
- **Adventure story:** The pupils write a short story entitled *Help!*, about a crisis, a call for help and a rescue. Discuss settings and scenarios together: e.g. *mountain rescue, man overboard.*
- **Playscript:** Ask the children to imagine that they are with a friend, when they discover an old bottle washed up on the beach. And there's a message inside! What will it say? Invite the children to write this out as a playscript, with names on the left and dialogue on the right.

Non-Fiction (Short task)
- **Poster:** Discuss together ways in which we all need help sometimes. How can we help our parents at home? Ask them to make a poster each for the classroom which offers guidance on how children can help out at home, e.g. *washing up,* or *tidying a bedroom.*
- **Directions:** People often need help when they are lost. Ask the children to pretend that a new neighbour asks them the way to the school. Can the pupils write a series of directions to lead their neighbour from home to school?

Non-Fiction (Long task)
- **Personal writing:** Ask the pupils to imagine they are being sent away to a remote island for a year. They may take three items with them. What will those three items be? Invite them to write a paragraph to explain why they would choose each item.
- **Information texts:** In pairs, the pupils choose (or are given) a particular remote island on a world map to explore. Using the Internet, encyclopaedias and other books, they must find out more about that island and present the information on paper, using text, pictures and maps.

Extension
- **Discussion text:** Ask the children to think about a time when they felt too embarrassed to ask for another person's help. How did they feel? Why were they unwilling to ask? Use these accounts to prompt a discussion about having the courage to ask for help.

Name _____ Date _____

EASY LIFE...

You are stranded, alone and hungry, on a desert island in the middle of the ocean. Your only chance of rescue is to send out a message in a bottle, and hope that someone finds it.

But what will you put? Write some words here and include a map of the island. Then all you can do is hope that someone finds it!

© Rising Stars UK Ltd. 2007   Mind's Eye/Writing   Year 3/MESSAGE IN A BOTTLE

Year 3/OFF-ROAD DRIVER

Introduction
- Where might this photograph have been taken?
- Why is this car driving through a river? Share theories and ideas together. Do the children think it might damage the vehicle? How?

Discussion
- Share knowledge and experience of driving through rivers and fords. Are most cars suited to this kind of driving? What make this car different?
- Share ideas about where this vehicle may be going and where it has come from. Could it be on rally of some kind, or an endurance race?

Interaction
- In pairs, share thoughts about what the driver and passengers may be thinking at this point. Are they worried about getting stuck? Encourage each pair to come up with some lines of speech to accompany this image.
- Hot seating: Invite volunteers to take turns in sitting in the 'hot seat' and fielding questions from the class in the role of the driver of the vehicle. Where is (s)he going?

Off-Road Driver © Imagebroker/Alamy

WORD BANK
- Invite the children to imagine that they have seen this vehicle just after it returns from wading through rivers and ploughing through mud. What does it look like? Encourage them to use interesting adjectives: e.g. *mud-encrusted, battered*.
- What other sorts of terrain might it be interesting to take this vehicle across? Invite the children to write down some ideas and then share them in class (e.g. snow drifts, swamps, desert).

WRITING ACTIVITIES

Fiction (Short task)
- **Postcard:** Invite the children to write their own fictional postcards home, after they have enjoyed a trek through the jungle in a vehicle like the one in the picture. What did they see? How did they feel?
- **Descriptive writing:** Ask the children to write a short descriptive paragraph about a time – either real or fictional – when they traveled through an odd place in a car. Ideas could include: *through a boggy field* or *across the desert*.

Fiction (Long task)
- **Adventure story:** Ask the pupils to plan and draft a story in which they go on an extraordinary journey in an off-road vehicle like the one in the photograph. What happens along the way? Do they get stuck?
- **Playscript:** In pairs, the children write a short script/conversation between the driver of this car and a passenger, as they enter the river. What will they say to one another? Act them out, sitting/driving the 4X4 in class.

Non-Fiction (Short task)
- **Personal writing:** Invite the children to think about what is their favourite type of vehicle. Is it a 4X4 like this one? Ask them to write a paragraph or two describing the vehicle and why they like it so much.
- **Warning poster:** Could any vehicle drive through a river like this? What would happen? Ask the children to design a poster which could be placed near to this river, warning other drivers not to attempt to drive through it (unless they have a 4X4!). Make particular use of exclamation marks.

Non-Fiction (Long task)
- **Promotional brochure:** Ask the children to imagine that they work for a new adventure holiday company that takes tourists on jungle treks and safaris. The pupils write a promotional leaflet, using ICT skills giving more information about the holidays: e.g. prices, where to stay, scenery, etc. Then share and appraise in class.
- **Magazine advertisement:** This time invite the children to imagine that they work for a 4X4 company. They have been asked to design and write a newspaper advert for an exciting new car that has just been made. They will need to show in the advertisement just what it can do!

Extension
- **Designs for the future:** What makes a good off-road vehicle? Ask the children to design and label a new type of off-road vehicle for the twenty-second century! What sort of features will it have? Invite the pupils to talk about their designs.

Name _____   Date _____

A MUDDY POEM

Can you imagine being in the off-road car as it trundles down the river?

Write a short poem in which you describe how it feels to be driving through a river instead of along a road! See if you can fit the following words into your poem.

- splashing
- wet windows
- muddy tyres
- frightening fish
- trundling
- jagged rocks
- watery shadows
- bubbles
- frothy foam

_____
_____
_____
_____
_____
_____
_____
_____

© Rising Stars UK Ltd. 2007   Mind's Eye/Writing   Year 3/OFF-ROAD DRIVER

Year 3/PARACHUTE JUMP

Introduction
- What is the name for this kind of equipment?
- Discuss together the design and colour of the parachute. Is it an old or new one? How can they tell? Who might be taking this photograph and from where?

Discussion
- Share knowledge of parachutes. How do they work? Has anyone seen a parachute in real life?
- Consider together why people might voluntarily make a parachute jump. Encourage the children to give reasons why they would or would not like to make a parachute jump.

Interaction
- Consider together where this person may land. Invite pupils to describe the landscape below him or her. For instance, is (s)he over a city or fields? Where would be the safest place to land?
- Encourage the children to share adjectives to describe this person's emotions, before, during and after the jump.

Parachute Jump © 1Apix/Alamy

WORD BANK
- Give some relevant examples of similes: e.g. *as light as a feather*. Then encourage the children, in small groups, to come up with some of their own similes for this picture, using ideas of e.g. nerves, freedom. Share ideas.
- Consider the word *parachutist* together. Can the pupils think of other jobs or pursuits that end in –ist? For example: *canoeist, pianist, florist, cellist* etc. Record these on the board.

WRITING ACTIVITIES

Fiction (Short task)
- **Descriptive writing:** Invite the children to imagine that they are the parachutist in the picture. Ask them to write a short paragraph describing the jump from beginning to end. Encourage them to describe the sights, sounds and feelings experienced.
- **Advertisement:** The children imagine they each work for a company that runs parachute jumps for beginners. They've been asked to produce a poster advertising the jumps. They share ideas and then make the poster, using colour, images and text and ICT if appropriate. Think about purpose and audience.

Fiction (Long task)
- **Story:** Ask the children to plan and draft their own stories in which someone makes their very first parachute jump. Describe the character's feelings the night before, on the morning of the jump and after it. How does the family feel? Would the parachutist do it again?
- **Playscript:** Ask the class to write a short conversation as a playscript, in which two or more jumpers are sitting in a plane, sharing their thoughts and feelings about the jump. Some are experienced, others are jumping for the first time.

Non-Fiction (Short task)
- **Personal writing:** Ask the children to complete the following line and then write a few sentences to give reasons for their choice.: *'If I could hover over anywhere in the world, I would choose…'* Share ideas in a plenary. Encourage the children to listen to others' choices.
- **Captions:** Ask each pupil to draw an illustration of a parachutist in full flight. Then ask them to think of some suitable captions to write underneath the picture – words which capture the mood and tone of the image. For example: *At last Man can fly like a bird!* or *Don't look down!*

Non-Fiction (Long task)
- **Newspaper report:** Explain to the class that they are roving reporters for a local newspaper. They have been sent to report on a giant charity parachute jump near their town. Ask them to report on, e.g. the weather, the crowds and the atmosphere, and to include some quotations from onlookers and jumpers.
- **Instructions:** Ask the children to write a series of imaginary instructions entitled *How to stay safe and enjoy your parachute jump.* Discuss the kinds of instructions that might be included, e.g. *relax, check your harness, don't look down.*

Extension
- **Information text:** Ask the children to research the subject of parachutes and jumping, using books in the library or Internet sites. Ask them to write this information up as a short information text, with pictures, diagrams, annotations and text.

Name _____   Date _____

DOWN WE GO!

Fill in the following spidergram, using all the verbs you can think of to describe how a parachutist may fall from the sky. Some examples have been included to get you started.

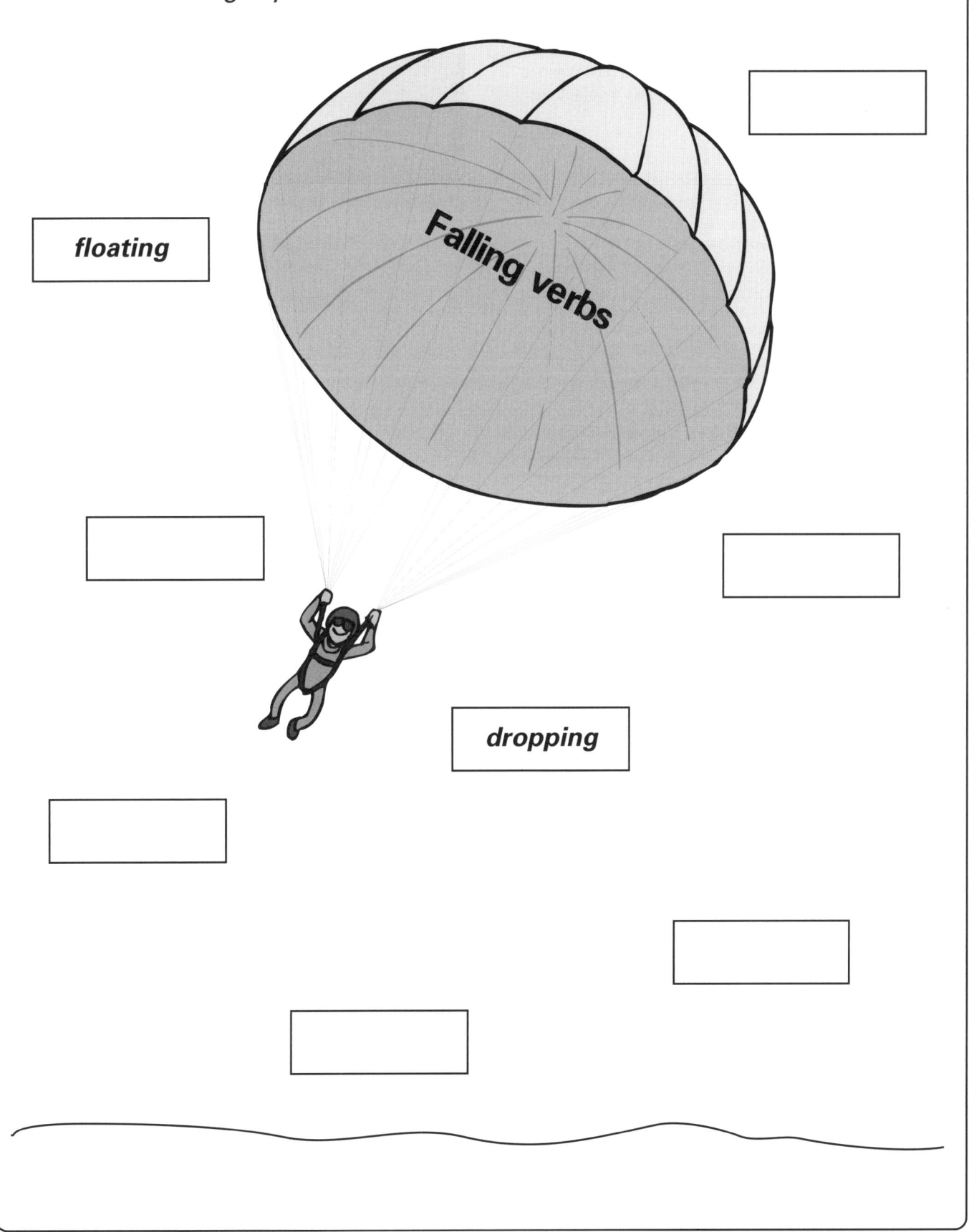

floating

Falling verbs

dropping

© Rising Stars UK Ltd. 2007   Mind's Eye/Writing   Year 3/PARACHUTE JUMP

Year 3/PARTY TIME

Introduction

- What can the children identify in the picture? Where was it taken?
- As a warm-up exercise, invite them to count the number of different colours they can see in the image. Share answers and count up together on screen.

Discussion

- Discuss together what might have been happening here. Was this photograph taken at a party? Elicit the children's knowledge and experience of parties, and the kinds of decorations people throw during parties.
- Consider together what is actually in the picture. Is it a table, or a carpet? Is this confetti, in which case when do people throw confetti?

Interaction

- In pairs, invite the children to come up with ideas about what has been happening in the scene. Share ideas in class.

- Word tennis: Remind the children of the many different colours featured in this image. Then play a word association game in which two people take turns to call out a new colour, until someone falters or repeats a colour.

Party Time © Westend61/Alamy

WORD BANK

- Check the spelling of all the colours the children can think of, either in groups or individually. Write the correct spellings on the board and address any common errors or confusion, e.g. *purple, orange, turquoise, violet* etc.
- Ask the children to think back to the parties they have attended. Can they describe the atmosphere? In pairs, invite them to write down words and phrases to describe the atmosphere at a party – e.g. *lively, exciting, happy, jolly, noisy, relaxed.*

WRITING ACTIVITIES

Fiction (Short task)

- **Descriptive writing (1):** Ask the children to write a paragraph or two describing the scene on the day of a party, just before the guests arrive. Think about the frantic activity, the food, the decorations and the excitement.
- **Descriptive writing (2):** Invite the children to write descriptive paragraph(s) again, but this time describing the scene and the atmosphere in the house after the party has finished and the guests have returned home. What does the house look like? How do they feel – e.g. *tired, full up*!

Non-Fiction (Short task)

- **Party invitation:** Ask the children to imagine they are holding a party soon – perhaps to celebrate a birthday, or for Halloween or Christmas. Ask them to prepare and design a party invitation that includes all the information their guests will need.
- **Recipe:** Discuss together the kind of food, drinks, decorations and games you might expect to find at a good party. Then encourage them to write all these things down as a 'Recipe for a Good Party'.

Fiction (Long task)

- **Story:** Ask the children to plan and draft a short story about a party that goes wrong in some way. Discuss ideas and plans together and then set the children writing. Remind them of the work they have already done on describing party atmospheres/scenery.
- **Wedding tale:** Discuss the idea that these streamers and confetti might have been used at a wedding reception. Then ask them to write a story or descriptive piece all about a fairy tale wedding. What will the bride and groom wear? How will they travel? What will the guests eat at the reception?

Non-Fiction (Long task)

- **Personal writing:** Invite the children to write about a party that they have enjoyed very much. Why was it so much fun? Encourage them to think about the sights, sounds and smells of the party! Refer back to the words banks above.
- **Thank you letters:** Discuss in class the importance of writing thank you letters to family and friends, both for attending your party, and, if you're lucky, for giving presents too. Discuss the layout of such a letter and then ask the children to draft one of their own, either real or fictional.

Extension

- **Design a poster:** Ask the children to design and produce a poster advertising a pretend party that is taking place soon. Encourage them to think about layout, colour, content and the key information that people will need to know.

Name _____ Date _____

A DREAM PARTY

If you could hold a dream party for your birthday, what would it be like? Where would it take place? How many would you invite, and what would you do?

Write down a description of your dream party in the space below. You will need to think about:

- venue (where it takes place)
- food and drink
- party games
- special surprises!

My Dream Party

_____
_____
_____
_____
_____
_____
_____
_____
_____
_____

Year 3/PYRAMIDS

Introduction
- In which country was this photograph taken? How can we tell?
- Elicit the children's knowledge and experience of the pyramids in Egypt. Do the children realise how close they are to the city? (You can see this clearly in the image.)

Discussion
- Discuss together where these riders may have come from and where they may be going. Discuss their clothing and head gear. Why is this kind of thing worn in the desert?
- Discuss the children's knowledge and experience of camels. Has anyone seen or even ridden one? Why are they so suited to a life in the desert?

Interaction
- What do the children think these riders may be saying to one another? Invite the pupils, in small groups or pairs, to come up with a line or two of speech to accompany this photograph. Then share in class.
- Hot seating: Invite volunteers to take turns in sitting in the 'hot-seat' and answering questions in the role of one of the camel riders in the image. Guide the children's questions to cover why they are there, where they are going, and what it feels like to live and work in such a hot and dry land.

Pyramids © medio images/Alamy

WORD BANK
- Remind the class that the word *pyramid* has a 'y' near the beginning that does not sound like a typical 'y', more like the 'i' in 'sit' for example. Can the children think of other similar words that have a 'y' near the beginning? E.g. *cylinder, cygnet*.
- The landscape in the picture is desert land. Invite the children to give other examples of landscapes around the world and brainstorm these on the board (e.g. *forest, arctic, mountainous*). For each one, ask the children to write down a list of adjectives to describe the landscape and climate – e.g. *desert: dusty, glaring, barren*.

WRITING ACTIVITIES

Fiction (Short task)
- **Pyramid poems:** Ask the children to write a poem in the shape of a pyramid (or triangle), with one word on the top line, two on the second, three on the third, and so on. The theme of their poems could be pyramids too.
- **Riddles:** As a whole class, write a short riddle for which the answer is 'a camel'. (E.g. *The hot sun gives me the hump, as my four legs sink into sand. What am I?*)

Fiction (Long task)
- **Short story:** Ask the children to plan and draft an original story written in the first person, from the viewpoint of a camel in the desert. What is their life like? What will happen to them?
- **Playscript:** Ask the children to write a short playscript in which two people enjoy a camel ride together through the desert. One is an experienced rider, the other is a very nervous beginner!

Non-Fiction (Short task)
- **Personal writing:** Ask the children to write a short paragraph describing how they might feel after spending one or two days in the desert. Then invite them to do the same for another landscape mentioned in the word bank.
- **Letter:** Invite the children to imagine that they have just enjoyed a ride across the desert, on a camel which they hired for the day. They write a short letter to the camel trader, thanking him for the use of his camel and describing their day.

Non-Fiction (Long task)
- **Non-chronological report:** Ask the pupils to find out more about camels and then put together their own information books on this topic. They should cover *where* they live, *what* they like to eat, *why* they have humps, *who* rides them, and so on.
- **Animal dictionary:** Ask the children to begin by writing a short definition of a camel. Discuss this in class. Then ask the pupils to compile their own animal dictionaries, including 10 other animals. Share definitions in a final plenary.

Extension
- **Explanation texts:** Set the children the task of writing a short piece in which they explain what a pyramid is to an alien who has never seen one before. They may have to explain what sand is first!

Name _____ Date _____

FUN WITH LETTERS

Alliteration is the name used for putting two or more words together that share the same first letter(s). For example: *crazy camels* or *dancing dolphins*.

See if you can think of some interesting adjectives (describing words) to put next to each of these amazing animals. Remember to choose words with the same first letters!

1. _____ **panther**

2. _____ **jelly fish**

3. _____ **lion**

4. _____ **kangaroo**

5. _____ **crocodile**

6. _____ **chimpanzee**

7. _____ **antelope**

8. _____ **fish**

9. _____ **sheep**

10. _____ **tiger**

11. _____ **fox**

12. _____ **snake**

© Rising Stars UK Ltd. 2007   Mind's Eye/Writing   Year 3/PYRAMIDS

Year 3/RACING DRIVER

Introduction
- Consider together what sort of car this is. Do you see them on the roads? Why not?
- Elicit the children's knowledge and experience of racing cars. Has anyone seen motor racing on television? Has anyone actually visited a track?

Discussion
- Discuss together why people race. What is it about speed that people find so thrilling? Would the children like to be racing drivers? Why, or why not?
- Consider together what sort of qualities one might need to become a good racing driver. Discuss the children's ideas and list any key words on the board: e.g. *strength, quick thinking*.

Interaction
- If the children could be any kind of sportsman or sportswoman, what would they be? Ask the children to think about this question in pairs, then feed back to the class, on behalf of their partners.
- Hot seating: Invite volunteers to come up to the 'hot seat' and answer questions in the role of the racing driver in the picture. What are they cheering about? Why do they enjoy racing so much?

Racing Driver © *Image 100/Alamy*

WORD BANK
- Working in pairs, the children write down a list of words to describe how it might feel to participate in a motor race. Share answers together and check spelling of key words on the board.
- Ask the children to write down all the other types of races they can think of, in which people are using something other than racing cars: e.g. *horse racing, motorbikes, quad bikes, bicycles*.

WRITING ACTIVITIES

Fiction (Short task)
- **Descriptive writing:** Ask the children to write a short description of the start of a motor race. They could either be in the car itself, or watching from the stands. Encourage them to think about the tension and the atmosphere. Refer them to their word banks.
- **Performance poem:** Ask the children to write a short poem to be performed aloud, in which they write about the different sounds of a motor race, e.g. *the roar of the engines, the cheering crowd, the screech of brakes*, etc.

Fiction (Long task)
- **Racing story:** Ask the children to plan and draft a short story about a motor race or other type of race. Perhaps something goes wrong, or they only realise they might win in the final lap.
- **Story about winning:** Invite the pupils to write a short story about winning; it could be a true story, or a fictional one. It may not involve a race; it could be a competition of some sort. Encourage them to consider the sequence of events that leads up to the competition.

Non-Fiction (Short task)
- **Personal writing:** Ask the children to think about their own favourite type of transport – it may be a racing car, or it may be a boat, plane, or hot air balloon, for example. Encourage them to give reasons for their choices.
- **Design and label:** Ask the children to make a sketch of a brand new type of racing car, fit for the twenty-second century. Alternatively, they may design a new racing driver's outfit. Remind them to use labels and captions.

Non-Fiction (Long task)
- **Personal writing:** Ask the children to write about their experiences of winning and losing – how it is important that we are able to do both politely and fairly. When have they lost and then felt frustrated and sad about it? Can we win every time?
- **Design a track:** Invite the pupils to design a brand new track or circuit – either for motor racing or for some other form of racing. Ask them to use labels for different parts of the circuit – e.g. sharp bends, ditches, water, etc.

Extension
- Ask the children to think about what their favourite sport is – to participate in or to watch. Why do they like it so much? Ask them to produce a short persuasive text in which they persuade readers to take up such a brilliant sport!

Name _____   Date _____

BEST CAR IN THE WORLD

What's your idea of the best car in the world? If you had all the money you ever wanted, what car would you buy – and why? Would it be a Formula One racing car, a Rolls Royce, a Ferrari, or something else?

Draw a sketch of your favourite car and then write a few sentences to explain why you like it so much! You may be able to find a picture of your favourite car which you can stick onto the page instead.

Name of car: _____

_____
_____
_____
_____
_____
_____

© Rising Stars UK Ltd. 2007   Mind's Eye/Writing   Year 3/RACING DRIVER

Year 3/RAINY STREET

Introduction
- What time of year could this be? Where was the picture taken?
- How many people can the children count in the photograph? Does anyone not have an umbrella? Who do they think is the wettest?

Discussion
- Elicit the children's experience of walking in the rain. How does it feel to get soaked through? Some people enjoy walking in the rain – why do you think this might be?
- Invite the children to come up with words and phrases to capture the thoughts of the people in this image. Share these in class, e.g. *I can't wait to get home*, etc.

Interaction
- Consider together how people tend to walk when they are out in the rain. Think about facial expressions too. In pairs, the children prepare and perform a short mime in which they get caught in the rain. Share these in class.
- In small discussion groups, invite the children to think about the way this country's weather is changeable and hard to predict. Would they like to live somewhere where it was always hot, or always cold? Share views.

Rainy Street © Dominic Burke/Alamy

WORD BANK
- Ask the children to make a list of the kinds of words to describe a rainy day like the one in the picture, e.g. *miserable, bitter,* etc. Then ask them to make another list of the feelings this kind of weather might cause us to have, e.g. *frustrated, damp, withdrawn.* Share these words in class.
- In pairs, the children write down all the types of weather they can think of, i.e. *rain, sunshine, snow* etc. Record these on the board and check spelling each time. These will be useful for the exercises below.

WRITING ACTIVITIES

Fiction (Short task)
- **Weather poem:** Invite the children to write a poem in which each stanza is describing a different type of weather, e.g. sun, rain, wind, snow. Encourage them to think about how it makes them feel inside. Refer to the words banks.
- **Descriptive writing:** Ask the children to choose an interesting place they have visited and write two short paragraphs: one to describe it in the rain, and another to describe how different it is in the sun.

Fiction (Long task)
- **Adventure story:** Invite the children to plan and draft an original short story in which heavy rain causes problems for the central characters – it may be e.g. a flood or a road closed. How will the characters cope?
- **Playscript:** In pairs, or individually, the children write a short playscript/dialogue in which two people get caught in the rain. One character hates the rain and wants to find shelter; the other loves being out in the rain and wants to stay longer.

Non-Fiction (Short task)
- **Rainy day poster:** Invite the pupils to design and produce a poster advising readers what to do on a rainy day! Share some ideas first, which may include: *modelling, watching a video, reading, cooking.*
- **Weather forecast:** Encourage the children to listen to/watch a weather forecast. Discuss the language used by the presenter. Then ask the children to write their own short forecast for the area in which they live. Encourage them to read/perform these to the class.

Non-Fiction (Long task)
- **Personal writing:** Ask the children to consider their favourite type of weather. Invite them to write a short piece in which they explain why they have chosen a particular type of weather. Options might include: *snow, sunshine, thunderstorm.*
- **Information text:** Rain may make us feel miserable sometimes, but it certainly has its uses! Invite the children to write/design an information page showing all the important uses of rain: e.g. watering crops, washing away dirt, etc.

Extension
- **Information text (2):** Ask the pupils to find out more about where rain comes from. They may use encyclopaedias, text books and the Internet. Ask them to present this information in a text (and oral presentation), using diagrams, sketches, labels and captions.

Name _____ Date _____

SOUNDS LIKE RAIN, AGAIN!

What does rain sound like? Have you ever been inside a tent, or a greenhouse during a heavy rain storm? It sounds wonderful!

Onomatopaiea is a term we use to describe words that show us the sound of things – like *splish-splash, or whiz, pop*!

Look at the words in the box below and then write a sentence for each one, showing the sound that rain makes.

| pitter-patter | splish-splash | gurgle | trickle | drip |

Some rainy sentences:

1. _____
   _____

2. _____
   _____

3. _____
   _____

4. _____
   _____

5. _____
   _____

© Rising Stars UK Ltd. 2007   Mind's Eye/Writing   Year 3/RAINY STREET

Year 3/ROBOT WORLD

Introduction
- How far into the future do the children think this image is set? How can we tell it is not today?.
- Encourage the children to share their knowledge and experience of fictional robot characters like the one in the picture. Is this a superhero or a villain? What equipment does he have, and what do we think it is for?

Discussion
- Discuss together what might be happening in this picture. Has the world been taken over by robots? Or is this figure half robot/half man?
- Look together at the background scene. Where is this set? Invite volunteers to imagine and describe the whole landscape, thinking about the debris on the ground and the blazing buildings above.

Interaction
- In pairs, the children come up with their own theories about when and where this is set, and what has happened. Share these in class.
- In pairs again, ask the children to think about what might happen next in this fictional world. Will the robot figure be attacked? Or has the battle ended?

Robot World © Smart.MAGNA/Alamy

WORD BANK
- Ask the children to write down the names (nouns) of all the things they can see in the picture (e.g. *car, building, flames,* etc.).
- Ask the children to refer back to the nouns above and put one or two interesting adjectives in front of each one (e.g. *mangled car, burning building, wrinkled pavement,* etc.).

WRITING ACTIVITIES

Fiction (Short task)
- **Storyboard:** Cartoons and other animated movies are usually made up of storyboards, onto which different scenes are placed. Ask the children to create a storyboard which includes this picture. They will then add a few preceding scenes or some that follow on.
- **Descriptive paragraph:** Say: Imagine you are the robot in the picture. Write a descriptive paragraph describing what you can see, hear, touch and smell. What has happened? Refer to the word bank.

Non-Fiction (Short task)
- **Design a robot warrior:** Referring to their word banks, ask the children to design their own robot warrior, with labels and captions. They will need to think about: costume, weapons, special skills – and a name! Then invite the pupils to present their work to the class, giving reasons for their choices.
- **Film advertisement:** Ask the children to imagine that the picture is actually a scene from a new action-cartoon film. Their task is to design a poster to advertise the film 'coming soon'.

Fiction (Long task)
- **Science-fiction story:** Ask the children to write their own short stories about the robot in the image. They will need to think about: setting, characters, and plot. Discuss possible ways of beginning the story.
- **Robot comic:** Ask the children to design and produce a comic (about four or five pages) about the adventures of the robot in the picture. Perhaps (s)he is a superhero?

Non-Fiction (Long task)
- **Battle report:** Ask the children to imagine that this robot is back at his head-quarters, after a long battle in the burning city. He has to write a battle report, to explain what happened. Ask the pupils to write this report. Share ideas first.
- **Newspaper headline:** Invite the class to imagine a newspaper report about what has happened in the picture. What would the headline be? *Robots defend city against aliens?* Discuss ideas together, and then encourage the children to write a news report of the scene.

Extension
- **Information text:** What do we know about robots? Can some robots really stand up and move around? Encourage the pupils to research the subject of robots and then produce a short information book, with pictures, diagrams, labels and captions.

Name _____ Date _____

WHAT CAN YOU SEE?

Look again at the picture. Do you think you could capture the sounds, sights and smells of the place in words?

Think about it. Then write a few sentences for each of the following senses. Try to imagine what it might be like to be in the picture, standing next to the robot warrior.

What can you see?

_____
_____
_____
_____

What can you hear?

_____
_____
_____
_____

What can you smell?

_____
_____
_____
_____

© Rising Stars UK Ltd. 2007   Mind's Eye/Writing   Year 3/ROBOT WORLD

Year 3/THE GIANT

Introduction

- How tall might this giant cowboy may be? Take guesses from the class. Focus on what may look like a telegraph pole at the bottom of the picture.
- Where do the children think this picture may have been taken? In America? How can we tell? Discuss the idea of the cowboy costume.

Discussion

- Discuss together what this statue may be for. Could it be advertising something – perhaps it is outside a cowboy grill house, or a shop that sells boots and hats?
- Elicit the children's knowledge and experience of cowboys and cowgirls. What do they do? Where do you find them in the world? Is there a difference between cowboys in films and the real cowboys still working today?

Interaction

- In pairs, ask the children to imagine what it must be like to be a giant, as tall as the cowboy in the picture, walking around the town. What would the buildings, cars and people look like? Ask them to make comparisons – e.g. the telegraph poles look like pencils, etc.
- In groups, the children discuss whether they would like to have been a cowboy in the early days of America. What would life have been like, on the move, camping under the stars? Would they have enjoyed it?

The Giant
© Vision of America, LLC/Alamy

WORD BANK

- Ask the pupils to think about the sorts of words one might find in a story about cowboys and cowgirls. In pairs, the children write these down in a list, and then feed back to the class. Examples to get them started are: *lasso, stirrup, saddles, Stetson, campfire, prairies*.
- Explain to the class about comparative and superlative adjectives: big, bigger, biggest. Remind them that a horse is big, an elephant is bigger, but the giant in the picture is the biggest! Encourage them to think of other comparatives and superlatives and write them down (e.g. *tall, taller, tallest*).

WRITING ACTIVITIES

Fiction (Short task)

- **Giant's cartoon comic:** Ask the children to include the image in a comic strip – on A4 paper – with six or nine small sketches, showing a story about a giant, with captions under each picture.
- **Poem:** Invite the children to consider again what it might be like to be a giant, entering a miniature world for the first time. Then ask them to write a short poem, either describing the giant, or describing what the our world looks like to a giant.

Non-Fiction (Short task)

- **Cowboy menu:** Invite the children to imagine that they are running a restaurant, selling cowboy style food: burgers, beans, etc. Ask them to design and write a menu for their cowboy restaurant. Encourage the children to include healthy main courses and delicious desserts for the hard-working cowboys.
- **Diary:** Ask the pupils to plan and draft a short extract from a 'giant's diary', describing what life is like, wandering through the miniature streets of your town.

Fiction (Long task)

- **Cowboy story:** Invite the class to write a story about cowboys and cowgirls, many years ago, driving cattle and sleeping under the stars. Encourage the children to use their word banks. Share story beginnings.
- **Giant story:** Ask the children to plan and draft a short story about a giant, who arrives in their home town. What is he doing there? Written in the first person, they could befriend the giant and lead him home.

Non-Fiction (Long task)

- **Personal writing:** Ask the children: if you could be a giant or a miniature person, which would you be, and why? Invite them to share their views in a short piece of personal writing, including a picture of them at the end.
- **Information book:** Ask the children to put together a short information text on the subject of cowboys and cowgirls. They could find out extra information from encyclopaedias and the Internet. Encourage them to focus on: where they come from, where they stay, what they eat, what they do.

Extension

- Ask the children to consider to whom *they* might seem like a giant – e.g. what must an ant think of them? Ask them to write a short story, set in the home of a tiny creature, which is disturbed by a giant visitor – the children!

Name _____   Date _____

GIANT STATUES

Have you ever seen another giant statue on your travels? Have you been holiday to a place where there is a giant figure in the town? What was it like?

Find out about famous statues across the world. You can use books, encyclopaedias and Internet sites. Draw a picture of four famous statues and then write about each one below.

FAMOUS STATUES OF THE WORLD

© Rising Stars UK Ltd. 2007 Mind's Eye/Writing Year 3/THE GIANT

Year 3/WATERFALL

Introduction

- Where do the children think this was taken? In this country or somewhere else? Discuss the lush green colours – could this be a tropical forest?
- Consider how many different colours the children can identify in this image. Ask them to count them up and then share answers.

Discussion

- Encourage the children to think of adjectives and abstract nouns to sum up how this picture makes them feel, when they imagine the landscape and the atmosphere.
- Discuss the kind of animals one might see in a place like this. Share these on the whiteboard together.

Interaction

- In pairs, the children take turns in closing their eyes and picturing themselves in the image. Their partner asks them questions about what they can see, hear, smell and so on. Key words could be recorded down on paper for use in the writing tasks below.
- In groups this time, encourage the children to share their knowledge and experience of waterfalls. Where have they seen them, and when? Can they describe the sound? How are waterfalls formed?

Waterfall © Jim Lundgren/Alamy

WORD BANK

- Discuss the idea of onomatopaiea with the children, giving examples (e.g. *whoosh, splash, pitter-patter*). Ask the children – either in pairs or groups – to write down all the onomatopoeic words they can think of that we might associate with water. Share these in a class plenary, and encourage the children to compile their own word banks.
- Set the children the challenge of seeing how many other words they can make from the letters that make up the word WATERFALL. Give the class two minutes to do this and then find out how many words they have made.

WRITING ACTIVITIES

Fiction (Short task)

- **Onomatopaiea poem:** Ask the children to write a short poem of their own in which they use as many 'watery' onomatopoeic words as they can, referring to their word banks.
- **Descriptive writing:** Ask the pupils to imagine they have been trekking through a tropical jungle like the one in the image. They are hot and thirsty, when suddenly they find the waterfall. Ask them to record in a few sentences how they feel when they see it, and then drink from it.

Non-Fiction (Short task)

- **Jungle quiz:** In pairs, ask the children to write a short quiz about the jungle for another pair of pupils. They could make use of the Internet or encyclopaedias when researching and compiling questions. Invite the pupils to exchange questions.
- **Diary entry:** Ask the pupils to write a short extract from an imaginary diary which records their trip through a tropical rainforest. One day they find a secret, magical waterfall in a clearing. Encourage them to narrate the events of the day in chronological order.

Fiction (Long task)

- **Rescue story:** Invite the children to write a short story in which someone has to be rescued after attempting to climb up the waterfall. How long will they have to wait? Will there be dangerous animals on the prowl?
- **Fantasy story:** What if the waterfall in the image had magical healing powers? Ask the children to write a short story in which some travellers stumble across a beautiful waterfall. One of them has been injured in the jungle, but is healed by the water.

Non-Fiction (Long task)

- **Persuasive brochure:** Ask the children to work in pairs to put together a short persuasive brochure advertising jungle trekking holidays. The children will need to think about prices, attractions and so on and consider together the purpose of the text, and the persuasive language.
- **Information books:** Ask the children to read books and encyclopaedias and/or research the Internet to find out some information about tropical rainforests. They may choose to focus on a particular aspect, e.g. rivers, and then produce a page or two of writing, pictures and diagrams.

Extension

- **Compound words:** It's easy to see where the word *waterfall* comes from – 'water' that 'falls' to earth over a cliff. This is a compound noun. Invite the children to list other compound nouns, e.g. *suitcase, football*. Perhaps they could then invent their own.

Name _____   Date _____

STRANGER IN THE JUNGLE

Imagine you are a wild animal that lives deep in the middle of a rainforest, like the one in the picture. You have never seen, heard or even smelled a human being before!

Suddenly you hear some noises, smell a strange scent in the air and see a very strange animal coming towards you through the bushes. It's a human...

Write down how you feel. Describe what this strange animal looks like to you.

_____

_____

_____

_____

_____

_____

_____

_____

_____

_____

_____

© Rising Stars UK Ltd. 2007   Mind's Eye/Writing   Year 3/WATERFALL

Year 3/CAVE ATMOSPHERE

Introduction
- Play the first few seconds of the clip. Invite the children to make guesses as to what might be making this strange sound.
- Play the entire sound clip. Then invite more suggestions. Discuss the idea of a cave. Share ideas about what could be making the 'ping' type sounds – establish too that there is water in the cave.

Discussion
- Elicit the children's knowledge and experience about underground caves. Has anyone visited one? Can they describe what the atmosphere was like, deep underground? Invite the others to close their eyes and imagine it.
- What does anyone know about echoes? How are they created? Play the clip again and listen out for echoes. Why do caves have so many echo sounds?

Interaction
- In pairs, invite the children to play a game in which they pretend to be one another's echo. Sitting opposite one another, they start with one or two words, with the echo coming straight back. Then encourage them to use longer phrases, with the echo beginning whilst the other is still speaking! Invite the pairs to share their work in front of the class.
- Replay the sound clip. In pairs once again, ask the children to take turns in describing what they think the interior of the cave looks like. These images may then be relayed back to the class, on behalf of each partner.

Audio clip
CAVE ATMOSPHERE (22 secs)

WORD BANK
- Play the sound clip again and then invite the children to come up with words that capture the sounds they hear on the piece – e.g. *drip, drop, ping,* etc. Introduce/revisit the term 'onomatopoeia'.
- Replay the sound clip again and then invite the children to 'say what they can see' in their mind's eye. Encourage them to find words and phrases that describe the features in the cave – e.g. *slippery, wet rocks, hollow cavern, crystal waters.*

WRITING ACTIVITIES

Fiction (Short task)
- **Cave poem:** Ask the children to compose their own poems set in a cave. Encourage them to refer to their word banks, and also to try to include references to echoes. Perform in class.
- **Descriptive paragraph:** Invite the pupils to write a short descriptive piece in which they describe an imaginary cave. Play the sound clip once again and refer back to the word banks for help.

Fiction (Long task)
- **Fantasy story:** Can the children imagine a dragon living in the cave? Play the clip again and encourage the children to picture the scene. Then ask them to draft a story in which some cavers stumble into a dragon's den.
- **Playscript:** Ask the children to write a short playscript/story dialogue in which three cavers are out caving together, when suddenly one of them gets trapped. How will they get him out?

Non-Fiction (Short task)
- **Personal writing:** Caves can be very interesting places to visit. But what is the most amazing place the children have ever visited, and why? Take some answers, and then ask the pupils to write about their chosen places in more detail.
- **Information poster:** Consider together the sort of creatures that may live in an underground cave. Use encyclopaedias, magazines and Internet sites to find out more. Then invite the children to produce information posters, showing labelled drawings of cave-dwelling creatures with captions.

Non-Fiction (Long task)
- **Travel recount:** Ask the children to imagine they are part of an expedition into this cave. Play the clip again, and encourage them to picture the scene. Then ask them to write an excerpt from a diary, in which they describe the scene and their progress.
- **Information book:** Help the children to find out more about caves. Use books, magazines and Internet sites. Then ask them to produce a short information text, with pictures, labels and captions.

Extension
- **Descriptive writing:** Ask the children to picture a whole palace underground. Can they imagine a king or queen who rules an underground world? Ask them to write a short piece, describing the cave-palace.

Name _____   Date _____

UNDERGROUND CITY

Imagine living underground! What would you see? What would you hear?

Pretend that you live in a giant cave many metres below the Earth's surface. What sort of things will you have in your cave? What will your furniture be like?

Draw a plan of your underground home and add some labels to show where everything is.

MY UNDERGROUND HOME

© Rising Stars UK Ltd. 2007   Mind's Eye/Writing   Year 3/CAVE ATMOSPHERE

Year 3/COUNTDOWN TO LIFT-OFF

Introduction

- Play the first few seconds of the clip. Invite the children to make guesses as to what is making this strange sound.
- Play the entire sound clip. Then ask the children to explain what is happening here. Where do they think the rocket is going?

Discussion

- Elicit the children's knowledge and experience of space travel. Play the clip again and focus on the words 'Apollo 11'. What do they know about this mission? It was this particular attempt that successfully reached the moon.
- What do we know about the moon? Share knowledge and display some fascinating facts on the board. You could find more information from books and Internet sites first.

Interaction

- Working in pairs, ask the children to role play this clip, re-enacting the countdown sequence and then playing out a dialogue between the NASA staff and the astronaut(s) on board. What might they say to one another?
- Hot seating: Ask for volunteers to sit in the 'hot seat' and field questions from the class in the role of the NASA crew at mission control, or one of the astronauts on Apollo 11.

Audio clip
COUNTDOWN (51 secs)

WORD BANK

- Invite the children to brainstorm the qualities you would need to be an astronaut. Discuss some words and phrases together first and then ask the pupils to get into pairs/small groups and then make a list of qualities, e.g. *courage, intelligence,* etc). Share these together in a final plenary.
- Consider together how these astronauts (and the ground crew) might feel during a countdown such as this. How would the children feel in their position? The pupils write down some words and share them in class.

WRITING ACTIVITIES

Fiction (Short task)

- **Rocket poem:** Ask the children to write a poem all about flying to the moon. How does it feel during the countdown? What does the moon look like, close up? How does it feel to be so far away from home?
- **Descriptive writing:** Invite the pupils to think about the scene on Earth at the launch pad, during the final countdown sequence. Play the clip again and encourage them to picture the control room, the launch, the crowds, etc. Then ask them to write a short piece, describing the scene.

Fiction (Long task)

- **Space story:** Ask the children to plan and draft a story in which a mission sets off, hoping to put humans on Mars for the very first time. Is the mission successful? What do they find when they get there?
- **Playscript/conversation:** Invite the pupils to write a short playscript/dialogue between the NASA control staff and the astronauts) on board Apollo 11 – during the lift-off, and then again during the touchdown on the lunar surface.

Non-Fiction (Short task)

- **Design a rocket:** Ask the children to design and label a brand new design for a rocket to travel to Mars. Share thoughts and then ask for volunteers to present their designs.
- **Equipment list:** What would you need to take with you on an expedition to the moon? The pupils make an equipment list for their first expedition into space. It is a long way, so they may need something to keep them occupied!

Non-Fiction (Long task)

- **Information text:** Encourage the children to find out more about Apollo 11 by using books, magazines and Internet sites. Then ask them to present this information in a two-page spread, with pictures.
- **Newspaper headline:** Ask the children to produce the front page of a pretend newspaper, reporting the story of the successful mission to land on the moon. Use ICT skills in typing, editing and redrafting the texts.

Extension

- **Personal writing:** Ask the children to consider whether they would like to go into space, like the astronauts of Apollo 11 on the sound clip. Why, or why not? The pupils write down their responses and explain their reasons.

Name _____ Date _____

POSTCARD FROM THE MOON

Imagine you are on the Apollo 11 space craft, as it lifts off into space.

Some days later you arrive at the Moon. Look around you. What do you see? What do you hear?

Write a postcard from the Moon to your family and friends back home!

Draw a picture on the front side and then write your message on the reverse, and the address of the person you are writing to.

GREETINGS FROM THE MOON

© Rising Stars UK Ltd. 2007 Mind's Eye/Writing Year 3/COUNTDOWN TO LIFT-OFF

Year 3/FIREWORKS

Introduction

- Play the first few seconds of the clip. What might be making this strange sound?
- Play the entire sound clip. Then ask the children to explain what is happening here. Can they hear the crowd present too? What occasion is this?

Discussion

- Elicit the children's knowledge and experience of fireworks. When are they usually used? Do the children celebrate Diwali? Do they know why we use fireworks on the 5th November?
- Share experiences of really good fireworks displays. Where have the children seen one? Does your school stage a fireworks display on Bonfire Night?

Interaction

- Working in pairs, the children share their likes and dislikes about Bonfire Night parties. What kind of fireworks are their favourites? Share feedback in class.
- In small groups, the pupil discuss ways of making sure Bonfire Night is a happy and safe experience. How do we handle fireworks safely? What can happen to us if we are not careful when around fires and fireworks?

Audio clip
FIREWORKS (08 secs)

WORD BANK

- Play the sound clip again and focus the children's attention on the gasps of the crowd, watching the fireworks display. Consider together the sort of noises we tend to make when we are impressed and surprised. Ask the children to make a list of these, e.g. *wow, gosh, ah!*
- What sort of noises do the fireworks themselves make? Remind the children about the idea of onomatopaiea again, and then consider some firework noises. Write these down and confirm the spellings, e.g. *whiz, pop, bang, fizz.*

WRITING ACTIVITIES

Fiction (Short task)

- **Fireworks acrostic poem:** Ask the children to plan and write an acrostics poem using the key word FIREWORKS. Remind them what an acrostic looks like, using a different key word (e.g. bonfire). Remind them to use their word banks for help.
- **Descriptive writing:** Play the clip again and ask the pupils to close their eyes and imagine they are at a firework display they remember. Then ask them to write about it, describing the sights, sounds and smells.

Non-Fiction (Short task)

- **Safety poster:** Ask the children to design and produce an A4 size poster, informing younger children how to keep safe when at a fireworks party. Discuss this together first.
- **Design a firework:** Encourage the pupils to come up with a design for their own brand new firework (named after them). They will need to think about what it looks like when you buy it, and the display that it produces in the sky. Their drawings will need to be labelled.

Fiction (Long task)

- **Story:** Ask the children to plan and draft a short story about Bonfire Night. Perhaps the rain comes and washes the fire out! Discuss possible storylines and then set them writing. Share story beginnings together in a plenary.
- **Story of Guy Fawkes:** Remind the children about the story of Guy Fawkes. Then ask them to put this story into a storyboard format, with several pictures on an A4 sheet, and space for some brief story narration and captions beneath.

Non-Fiction (Long task)

- **Information text:** Ask the children to produce a short information text all about fire. How is it made? What are the many uses we have for fire? The children present their work to the class, talking about their choice of language and design.
- **Personal writing:** Invite the children to write a short piece in which they give their own views about Bonfire Night. Do they enjoy it? What do they like/dislike about fireworks parties? Have they ever been frightened by fireworks?

Extension

- **Names of fireworks:** Invite the children to come up with a list of names and descriptions for some brand new fireworks. Discuss possible names together, to get them started, e.g. *Whizpopper, Crackerjack,* etc. Refer the pupils to their word banks.

Name _____   Date _____

COME TO OUR FIREWORKS PARTY!

Imagine you are holding a fireworks party to celebrate the 5th November.

Design an attractive poster to advertise your party. Don't forget to think about:

- the date
- the time
- the place
- the entertainment

© Rising Stars UK Ltd. 2007

Mind's Eye/Writing   Year 3/FIREWORKS

Year 3/HORSE RACE

Introduction
- Play the first few seconds of the clip. Invite the children to suggest who is speaking here. What is the occasion?
- Play the entire sound clip. Invite more suggestions from the children. Discuss the strange names mentioned and terms like 'furlong'.

Discussion
- Establish that this is the commentary for a horse race. Replay the clip and list the names of the horses featured. Then try to establish the finishing order of the horses, including the photo finish between the two front runners.
- Elicit the children's knowledge and experience of horse racing. Have they seen it on television? Has anyone been to a horse race? Can they describe it for the class?

Interaction
- Working in pairs or small groups, ask the children to discuss other spectator sports. The pupils list these on a large sheet of paper and then feed back to the class in a plenary. Which of these examples are the most popular within the class?
- In pairs, the children take turns to be this commentator and narrate an imaginary horse race. Can they build the tension and excitement as the race reaches its end? Share performances and discuss: speed of delivery, tone and expression.

Audio clip
HORSE RACING (26 secs)

WORD BANK
- Ask the pupils to make a list of words and phrases to describe the atmosphere at this event, as the clip is replayed again. Share these words in class.
- In pairs, the children make a list of all the nouns they can think of that might be associated with horse racing (e.g. *jockey, stable, stirrup, fence*). Check spelling together on the board.

WRITING ACTIVITIES

Fiction (Short task)
- **Rhythmic poem:** Discuss the sounds of a horse race. Focus on the regular beat of the horses' hooves. Then think together how this could be conveyed in a poem. Model some lines on the board and then set the pupils the task of writing a poem about horse racing. Invite them to perform these poems; think about expression, tone and volume.
- **Descriptive writing:** Play the clip again, then encourage the children to write a short descriptive piece in the role of one of the jockeys in the race. Describe the sound, feel, sights and smells of the race.

Fiction (Long task)
- **Racing story:** Invite the children to write a short story in the first person, as the rider, or owner, of *Running Fence*. Narrate their day, from when they get up to the result of the photo finish. Who really won in the end?
- **Animal story:** Remind the children that animal stories are often written in the role of the animals – seeing the world through their eyes. This time, the children are going to write a story about the race featured in the sound clip, writing in the role of one of the horses.

Non-Fiction (Short task)
- **Design an outfit:** Consider together what riders tend to wear in horse races. Their tunics and hats are often brightly coloured so that they can be easily identified. Invite the children to design a brand new outfit for a jockey, with matching tunic and hat. Label the designs.
- **Advertisement:** Ask the pupils to design an advertisement for a day at the races. They will need to think about the date, venue, times and races on offer. They could include the other attractions you can find at a racecourse – e.g. restaurants and television screens. Explore together how texts of this kind can appeal to readers.

Non-Fiction (Long task)
- **Letter:** Imagine that in the end it was *Blue Jack* who won the race in that photo finish with *Running Fence*. Ask the children to write a letter, from the owner of the *Blue Jack* to the horse's jockey, congratulating him (or her) on a glorious victory.
- **Racing interview:** Invite the pupils to write a short interview between the winning jockey and a sports commentator, just after the race, when the news comes through that (s)he won the photo finish. How do they feel?

Extension
- **Personal writing:** Invite the children to think about which sport they most enjoy watching. Ask them to write about why they think it makes such a good sport to watch. Focus on the clarity and consistency of handwriting.

Name _____ Date _____

UNUSUAL NAMES!

Have you ever seen or heard a horse race in action? If you have, you will know that the horses are often given quite unusual names, like Blue Jack, Mickey's Girl and Little Poppet.

Can you think of some interesting names for these horses?

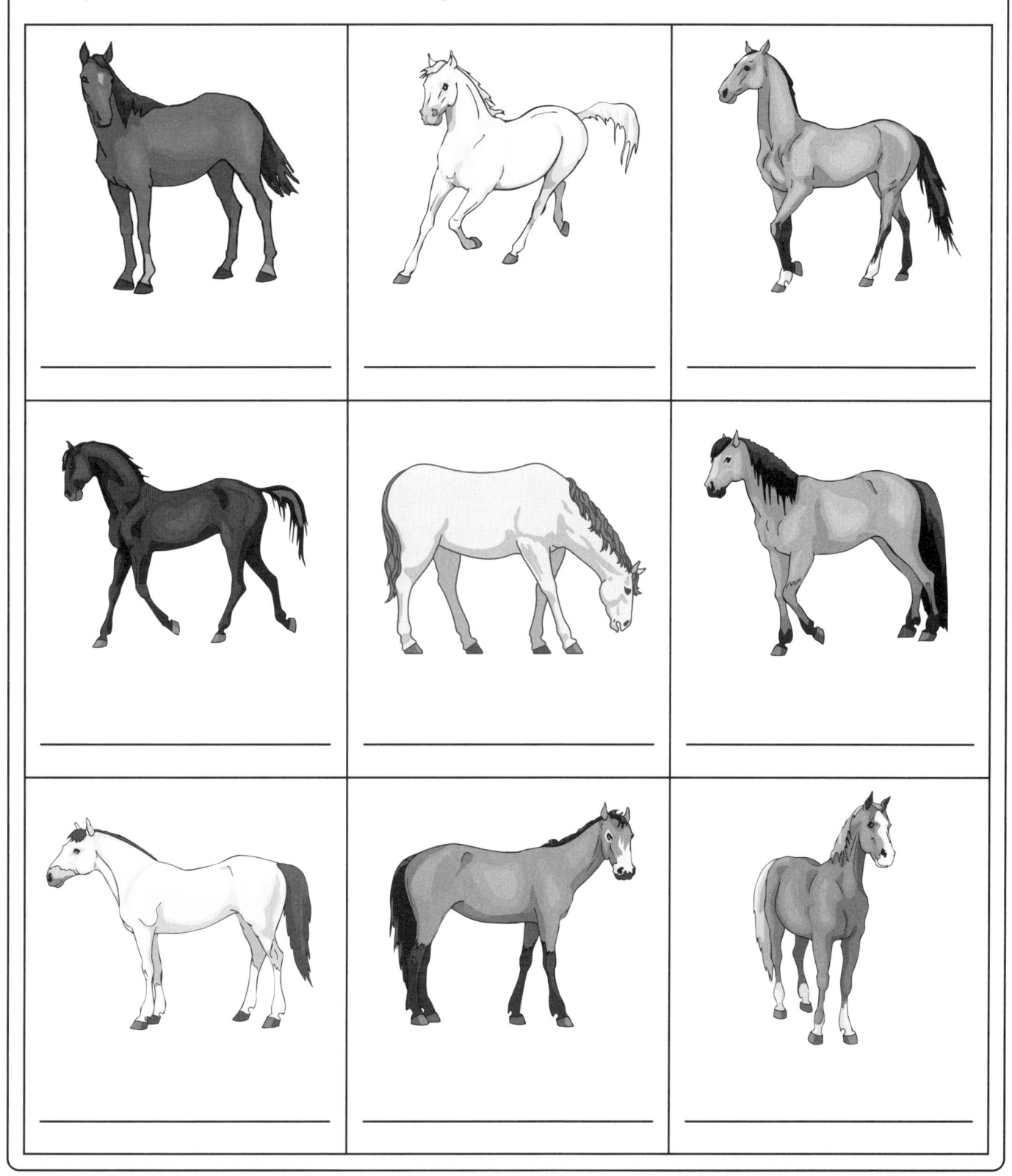

© Rising Stars UK Ltd. 2007　　　　　　　　　　　　　　　　　Mind's Eye/Writing　Year 3/HORSE RACE

Year 3/JUMBO JET

Introduction

- Play the first few seconds of the clip. Is this the sound of some sort of machine? An engine, perhaps?
- Play the entire sound clip. Invite more suggestions from the children as to the origins of this sound.

Discussion

- Elicit the children's knowledge and experience of aeroplanes – and particularly jumbo jets. Has anyone travelled on one or seen one? Listen to the children's anecdotes.
- Play the clip once again. Can anyone think who it is who might be speaking here? (i.e. the pilots/control tower. Can the children identify what they are saying?

Interaction

- In pairs, ask the children to prepare a short role play in which they are sitting side by side, as the sound clip runs (i.e. they are passengers on a jumbo jet, as it takes off). One of them could be quite nervous about the flight (first time etc.), while the other is enjoying it.
- In pairs again, encourage the children to prepare another short role play in which one person is the pilot of the plane and the other is a member of staff in the control tower. What might they say to one another as the plane takes off?

Audio clip
JUMBO JET (49 secs)

WORD BANK

- Ask the children to make a list of words to describe how they feel when they are flying. If some have never flown, invite them to imagine how they would feel. Share these words and phrases in class, looking for common feelings and some surprises.
- Ask the children if there are ever moments in their lives when they feel just like the jumbo jet, gathering power and speed ready to burst away, or into something – e.g. running races, dancing, etc. Encourage them to write these down and then share them in class.

WRITING ACTIVITIES

Short task — Fiction

- **Poem:** Ask the children to plan and compose a poem all about flying. It could be about when they themselves have flown, or about the aeroplane itself, as it soars through the air. You may wish to introduce/revise similes here.
- **Descriptive writing:** Ask the children to write a short piece describing an interesting journey that they have been on – it could be a plane flight, or some other form of travel.

Short task — Non-Fiction

- **Personal writing:** What do the children know about aeroplanes? Ask them to write down everything they know and include a picture of a jumbo jet. They could do research in books and magazines to find out more.
- **Design a new aeroplane:** What will planes look like in two hundred years time? Encourage the pupils to design a new plane, fit for the future, and label it to show all its features.

Long task — Fiction

- **Adventure story:** Ask the children to plan and draft a short story about an exciting aeroplane flight. Perhaps it is an especially long flight to the other side of the world. Share ways of beginning the story – perhaps starting with the take off.
- **Dialogues/playscripts:** Remind the children of their role play. Ask them to create a short playscript or simple story dialogue between two passengers on a plane. Perhaps one of them is nervous, while the other one is excited. Or perhaps they are two old friends who find themselves sitting next to one another.

Long task — Non-Fiction

- **Personal writing:** Ask the children to write a recount about a real or imaginary plane trip. Remind them to use connectives such as 'Once we were at the airport...', and 'Two hours later...'.
- **History project:** How has flight changed over the years? How have aeroplanes evolved? Using books, encyclopaedias, magazines and Internet sites, ask the children to put together a presentation (on paper or using PowerPoint/pictures) on the history of the aeroplane.

Extension

- **Personal writing:** Ask the children: *If you owned your own private jet plane where would you go, and why?* Encourage them to write down their thoughts in a piece of formal writing. They may include a picture of their jet (or their destination).

Name _____ Date _____

COULD YOU FLY AN AEROPLANE?

What do you think you need to be a good airline pilot? Think about it.

Draw a picture of a pilot, behind the controls of an aeroplane, and then write down some words and phrases below it to describe what sort of person he or she may be.

You could start with: *clever, good eyes, calm, friendly*.

To be a good pilot you must be _____

_____

_____

_____

_____

© Rising Stars UK Ltd. 2007   Mind's Eye/Writing   Year 3/JUMBO JET

Year 3/RING THE ALARM!

Introduction

- Play the first second or two of the sound. Encourage the children to guess what is happening.
- Play the whole sound effect. Share responses again. Establish that it is some sort of alarm. But what type of alarm, and why is it going off? Share theories.

Discussion

- Elicit the children's knowledge and experience of alarms. Have they heard an alarm like this before? Discuss the school's fire alarm system. Does it sound like this?
- Discuss together how we feel when we hear alarms ringing like this. Encourage the pupils to volunteer words and phrases and write these on the board, e.g. *nervous, confused, determined.*

Interaction

- In pairs, the pupils come up with theories about what has happened in the sound clip – why the alarm is ringing and what happens next. Then invite each pair to give feedback, as the sound is playing.
- In pairs, ask the children to make a list of all the different types of alarms they can think of – from burglar alarms to smoke alarms. Share these in class. Can the children imitate the different sounds?

Audio clip
BURGLAR ALARM (59 secs)

WORD BANK

- Drawing on earlier discussions, encourage the children to write down all the feelings that an alarm can conjure up in us, checking to spell each word correctly. These will come in useful in writing projects below.
- Can the children put different alarm sounds into words? How would we write the sound of an alarm in a story or poem? E.g. *ring-ring, beep-beep.* Discuss the concept of onomatopaiea together.

WRITING ACTIVITIES

Fiction (Short task)

- **Alarm poem:** Play the sound clip again. Then ask the children to compose a short poem all about alarms – what they sound like, and how they make us feel. They should refer to their word banks, and include onomatopoeia.
- **Descriptive writing:** Play the clip once more. Ask the children to close their eyes and imagine a scene, as the alarm goes off. Ask them to write a descriptive paragraph or two describing the scene they can see, e.g. people rushing out of a hotel or school; a shop with a flashing light outside.

Fiction (Long task)

- **Story:** Ask the children to plan and draft a short story in which an alarm is rung to signal an emergency. What has happened to cause the alarm? How is the emergency dealt with?
- **Story:** Ask the pupils to plan and draft a short story in which an alarm is accidentally (or intentionally) set off several times – i.e. false alarms. Then, when it is set off because there is an emergency, no one believes it is real... What happens next?

Non-Fiction (Short task)

- **Instructions:** Ask the children to compose a set of instructions about 'what to do in case of a fire'. Discuss the best safety precautions together and then encourage them to write these down as bullet points, perhaps including illustrations.
- **Personal writing:** Have the children ever been in a place when an alarm has rung? Ask them to write about their experiences.

Non-Fiction (Long task)

- **Information book:** Ask the children to produce a two-page information text all about alarms. They could cut out pictures from magazines or print them off from the Internet. Then write a little about each type.
- **Personal writing:** Remind the class how our emergency services are often the only people going into a building when everyone else is being evacuated out. How must this feel? Ask the children to write about how it would feel to be a police officer or fire fighter, going to an emergency, just as others are running away from it.

Extension

- **Personal writing:** In the days before electric alarms were invented, what did people use? Ask the children to write their views on what people must have done to put an urgent message across (e.g. beat a drum, ring a bell).

Name _____ Date _____

WHAT SHALL WE DO?

Imagine that you and a friend are out shopping, or visiting the cinema, when you both hear an alarm sound. One of you believes this is just a joke – a false alarm caused by someone who has set off an alarm for fun. The other person thinks it is real and that you should leave quickly.

Write down a conversation you might have together, each of you trying to persuade the other you are right!

Sound of alarm suddenly starts to ring.

1st person _____
_____

2nd person _____
_____

1st person _____
_____

2nd person _____
_____

1st person _____
_____

2nd person _____
_____

© Rising Stars UK Ltd. 2007   Mind's Eye/Writing   Year 3/RING THE ALARM!

Year 3/RIVER FLOWING

Introduction
- Play the first few seconds of the clip. Invite the children to make guesses as to what might be making this sound.
- Play the entire sound clip. Then invite more suggestions as to what could be making the sound. Establish that it is the sound of a river flowing.

Discussion
- Elicit the children's knowledge and experience of rivers. Is there a river in your locality? What is it like? Where does it come from and where does it lead to?
- Have any of the children enjoyed a holiday on river? What was it like? Would anyone else enjoy such a boat trip? Why do many of us like rivers so much?

Interaction
- Play the clip once again and then invite the children to get into small groups and imagine that they are enjoying a picnic near the river. Can they work out a two-minute role play, in which they enjoy splashing about or fishing in the river? Play the sound clip as each group performs their role play.
- Ask the children, in small groups or pairs once again, to write down the names of all the rivers they can think of. They may be anywhere in the world. Share feedback and then establish where each river is located. (You could use atlases and maps.)

Audio clip
RIVER SOUND (31 secs)

WORD BANK
- Ask the children to come up with some useful words and phrases to describe a river: its sound, how it feels, what it looks like and so on. E.g.: *full of life, cool and refreshing*.
- Invite the children to think of all the sorts of things you can do in a river, and to write these down in a list. Check the spelling of these words and phrases in a class plenary, e.g. *swimming, diving, cruising, fishing, fly fishing*, etc.

WRITING ACTIVITIES

Fiction (Short task)
- **River poem:** Ask the children to compose a poem each about a river, e.g. the wildlife found in it, the sorts of things it flows past, the sound it makes. Brainstorm key words and phrases first, and refer back to the pupils' word banks.
- **Descriptive paragraph:** Invite the children to write a descriptive piece about a river that they know. It may be one they live near, or one they have visited on holiday. Encourage them to describe the sights, sounds and smells, and how they feel when they are there.

Fiction (Long task)
- **Fantasy story:** Ask the children to write a story about a magic river, that leads you to a fantastic place – perhaps a castle, or through a magic forest, or to another world. Describe the river – is it blue? Does it glitter and sparkle?
- **River journey:** Invite the children to plan and draft a short story/fictional recount about a special boat trip through the Amazon rainforest, or along the River Nile. Share ideas about what they might see along the way.

Non-Fiction (Short task)
- **Boat trips:** Ask the children if they have ever enjoyed a boat trip, or a fishing trip, on a river. Then set them the task of creating an advertisement (A4 poster size) for trips on a local river. They will need to think about, e.g. ticket prices, location, attractions, wildlife.
- **Safety instructions:** Discuss with the children the important ways of keeping safe when near rivers, e.g. keeping an adult with you, never going out of your depth, etc. Suggest that they put these points into a poster, informing younger children how to keep safe near rivers.

Non-Fiction (Long task)
- **Personal writing:** Discuss together why so many people like being on or near rivers. What is about water that we find so appealing? Play the clip again and discuss why so many of us find the sound of water relaxing and peaceful.
- **Information book:** Invite the children, working in pairs, to put together a short information book/page-spread on a particular famous river of the world – e.g. *Nile, Amazon, Thames, Seine*. Think about the places it runs through, and how it serves the people and animals along the way.

Extension
- **Explanation text:** Discuss together what the children know about how rivers are formed. Then invite them to put together a simple explanation text, using drawings and labels, showing where the water comes from and where it leads to.

Name _____ Date _____

A VILLAGE ON WATER!

Just think how many different animals all live on, in and beside a river! Think about the times you have visited a river. What sort of wildlife did you see?

Using books, magazines and some websites, find out what sort of animals are at home in rivers. Then draw a picture of each animal and write about it underneath.

© Rising Stars UK Ltd. 2007　　　　　　　　　　　Mind's Eye/Writing　Year 3/RIVER FLOWING

Year 3/ROYAL FANFARE

Introduction

- Play the first few seconds of the clip and then invite suggestions as to what it may be, and what may follow.
- Then play the whole sound clip. Elicit the children's initial responses to it. Could this be a royal fanfare? If so, who could be arriving?

Discussion

- Elicit the children's knowledge of musical instruments and orchestras. Can anyone identify the instruments that feature in the sound clip? Re-play the clip several times and see if you can name all of them together.
- If this is not a royal fanfare, then what else could be happening? Share ideas around – e.g. *unveiling of something, arrival of special guest, boat launch.*

Interaction

- Working in pairs, or small acting groups, the children prepare a short scene to play out as the sound clip is heard. They will need to think of a special event, with one of them narrating the scene as though for television.
- In small discussion groups, encourage the children to discuss their responses to the question: *If you could have any special guest visit the school, who would it be, and why?*

Audio clip
DANCING GIRL (20 secs)

WORD BANK

- Can the children imagine they are a monarch or some other VIP, arriving at a special ceremony? How do they feel then? Encourage them to write down some key words and phrases, e.g. *regal, important, beautiful, nervous, excited.*
- Is there a pattern emerging in the fanfare? Can the pupils count the number of blasts and bangs? Discuss words like '*peep, parp, bang, ring*'. Invite them to experiment with ways of converting the fanfare into words, so it is recognisable.

WRITING ACTIVITIES

Fiction (Short task)

- **Descriptive writing**: Ask the children to imagine that the fanfare is to welcome the arrival of a member of royalty to a banquet. Ask them to write a descriptive paragraph or two in the first person, in the role of a royal servant or footman.
- **Poem about a king or queen**: Invite the children to use the sound clip to help them picture a queen or king in their minds. What does (s)he look like? What is their character like? Ask the pupils to write a poem describing their chosen king or queen. Refer to the word banks.

Non-Fiction (Short task)

- **Royal banquet**: Invite the children to imagine that the music on the sound clip is welcoming the guests to a great royal banquet. But what is on the menu? Lobster? Venison? Giant chocolate gateau? Ask the children to design and produce a beautiful menu for the royal feast. Share ideas.
- **Design a costume fit for a king or queen**: Ask the pupils to design and label a costume for a king or queen to wear to such a royal banquet. Perhaps this is a very young monarch, so the costume needs to be fashionable as well as grand!

Fiction (Long task)

- **Story**: Invite the children to plan and draft a short story about a royal wedding – either today or many years ago. Encourage them to describe all the frantic preparations, the cooking and decorating, ready for the big day.
- **Fairy tale/traditional story**: Ask the children to have a go at writing their own fairy tale, inspired by the royal fanfare on the sound clip. It could be set in a great castle or tower. Perhaps a young princess is feeling lonely – and then a prince arrives!

Non-Fiction (Long task)

- **Day in the life of the Queen**: Ask the children to prepare an extract from a fictional diary kept by a king or queen. What did they do today? Discuss together the kinds of daily duties every monarch has – e.g. receiving visitors, visiting special events, etc.
- **Magazine article**: Ask the pupils to design and write the front page of an imaginary newspaper, reporting the story of a great royal wedding. They will need to think of a headline, some pictures, and lots of description and comments.

Extension

- Play the clip again and then encourage the children to find out more about the instruments in the clip (e.g. trumpet, bugle, cornet). Ask them to put together a short information text, showing the differences between these instruments.